JANUA LINGUARUM

STUDIA MEMORIAE
NICOLAI VAN WIJK DEDICATA

edenda curat
C.H. VAN SCHOONEVELD
Indiana University

Series Practica, 180

A Sketch of Comparative Dravidian Morphology:

Part One

Kamil Zvelebil

Mouton Publishers
The Hague · Paris · New York

ISBN 90 279 7646 5

Printed in the Netherlands

Dedicated to
Murray Barnson Emeneau

PREFACE

"Dravidian philology and comparative grammar have not yet reached the stage when the student can go to a convenient set of handbooks when he wishes light on points of morphology" (M. B. Emeneau, "Some South Dravidian Noun Formatives", *Ind. Linguistics* 27 [1966], issued Sept. 1968], 21).

"Compared to the progress made in the area of comparative phonology, work done in comparative morphology is frustratingly meagre and slow" (Bh. Krishnamurti, "Comparative Dravidian Studies", *Current Trends in Linguistics, 5: Linguistics in South Asia* [1969], 318).

This short account of the surface structure of Dravidian morphology is intended to be a preliminary text which should be useful for quick typological orientation of those who wish to have a first and very fundamental acquaintance with Dravidian structure. Therefore, any specific theoretical bias has been as much as possible avoided, and the account is given in rather traditional terms and in a simple and brief manner. It is hoped that it will at least in part fill the gap felt by the students referred to above in the quotation from Emeneau, to whom this book is humbly dedicated.

KAMIL ZVELEBIL

Kern Institute
University of Leiden
1971

TABLE OF CONTENTS

List of Abbreviations xi

Introduction 3

1. Nouns 9
   1.1 Substantives 9
   1.2 Numerals 33
   1.3 Pronouns 36

2. Adjectives 59
   2.1 Definition and use 59

Bibliography 71

Index 75

LIST OF ABBREVIATIONS

Bad.	=	Badaga
Br.	=	Brahui
C	=	Consonant
CDr	=	Central Dravidian
CDG	=	Robert A. Caldwell, *A Comparative Grammar of the Dravidian or South-Indian Family of Languages* (1856, 1875, 1913).
CKa.	=	Colloquial Kannada
coll.	=	colloquial
CT	=	Colloquial Tamil
DBIA	=	M. B. Emeneau and T. Burrow, *Dravidian Borrowings from Indo-Aryan* (Berkeley, 1962).
DED	=	M. B. Emeneau and T. Burrow, *A Dravidian Etymological Dictionary*, (Oxford, 1961).
DEDS	=	M. B. Emeneau and T. Burrow, *A Dravidian Etymological Dictionary-Supplement* (Oxford, 1968).
DEDS S	=	*A Dravidian Etymological Dictionary-Supplement*, entries S 1-S 889.
DJ	=	M. S. Andronov, *Dravidijskije jazyki* (Moskva, 1965).
DL	=	*Dravidian Linguistics* (Seminar Papers), ed. S. Agesthialingom and N. Kumaraswami Raja (Annamalainagar, 1969).
Dr.	=	Dravidian
Eḻut.	=	*Tolkāppiyam - Eḻuttatikāram*
EM	=	A. C. Sekhar, *Evolution of Malayalam* (Poona, 1953).
Ga. (Oll.)	=	Gadba (Ollari)
Ga. (S.)	=	Gadba (Salur)
Go.	=	Gondi
Hi.	=	Hindī
HTL	=	T. P. Meenakshisundaran, *A History of Tamil Language* (Poona, 1965).
IA	=	Indo-Aryan
IHGTL	=	K. Zvelebil, Yu. Glazov, and M. Andronov, *Introduction to the Historical Grammar of the Tamil Language* (Moscow, 1967).
Ir.	=	Irula
Ka.	=	Kannaḍa
Ko.	=	Kota
Koḍ.	=	Koḍagu
Kol.	=	Kolami
Kur.	=	Kuru<u>kh</u>
Kuṟ.	=	*Kuṟuntokai*
LKa.	=	Literary Kannaḍa
lit.	=	literary
LSI	=	*The Linguistic Survey of India* iv (Calcutta, 1906).
LT	=	Literary Tamil
Ma.	=	Malayalam
Malt.	=	Malto
Manḍ.	=	Manḍa
NDr	=	North Dravidian

Nk.	=	Naikṛi, a dialect of Kolami
Nk. (Ch.)	=	Naiki of Chanda
OKa.	=	Old Kannaḍa
OMa.	=	Old Malayaḷam
OTa.	=	Old Tamil
OTe.	=	Old Telugu
Pa.	=	Parji
PCDr	=	Proto-Central Dravidian
PDr	=	Proto-Dravidian
Pe.	=	Pengo
PGT	=	H. Beythan, *Praktische Grammatik der Tamilsprache* (Leipzig, 1943).
Pkt.	=	Prakrit
PSDr	=	Proto-South Dravidian
Puṟ.	=	*Puṟanāṉūṟu*
s.	=	*sūtra*
SDr	=	South Dravidian
SGD	=	J. Bloch, *Structure grammaticale des langues dravidiennes* (Paris, 1946).
Skt.	=	Sanskrit
Ta.	=	Tamil
Te.	=	Telugu
Tiruk.	=	*Tirukkuṟaḷ*
To.	=	Toda
Tolk.	=	*Tolkāppiyam*
Tolk. Col.	=	*Tolkāppiyam, Collatikāram*
Tu.	=	*Tuḷu*
TVB	=	Bh. Krishnamurti, *Telugu Verbal Bases* (Berkeley, 1961).
V	=	Vowel

NOTE

A bibliography on Dravidian morphology will be appended to the last part of the *Sketch* (on word-formation).

Part One

NOUNS AND ADJECTIVES

INTRODUCTION*

0.1 As to their 'surface' and 'phonetic' structures,[1] Dravidian languages, generally speaking, would probably be called *agglutinative* in the terms of Schlegel and Finck. However, some features of "internal flexion"[2] are present, not to speak of morphophonemic alternations in the vowel and consonantsquantities within the roots.[3] The elements of internal flexion though, are rather rare and seem to have only marginal importance; also, they do not seem to be widely and systematically spread throughout the entire family. Nevertheless, it would not be correct to entirely ignore them.[4]

0.2 *Suffixation* is the only type of affixation which occurs in Dravidian.[5] Consequently, the root-morpheme stands always as the first morpheme of a word (in the linear order from left to right).

0.3 All Dravidian roots are *monosyllabic*. Though the monosyllabicity of Dr. roots is until this day only a hypothesis, it works extremely well; and it seems that ultimately monosyllabic roots will have to be reconstructed for Proto-Dravidian as facts of Dr. structure.[6]

Root-syllables can be *open* (vowel-ending) or *closed* (consonant-ending), *long* or *short*. The specific syllabic pattern ('canonical form') of Dravidian in terms of V and C in roots is thus $(C_1)\ \breve{\bar{V}}\ (C_2)$. *Consonants clusters* seem to have occurred originally only on morph-boundaries.

Any short or long radical vowel (i.e. *ī̆, *ū̆, *ē̆, *ō̆, *ā̆) may occur within the root. The character of C_1 depends on the phonetic restrictions on the occurrence of consonants in the particular language in question (i.e. any consonant occurring in the initial position may equal C_1). Any consonant with the possible exception of *ñ occurs as C_2.

In PDr., no consonant of the alveolar and the cacuminal-retroflex series, i.e. *ṯ, *ḻ, *ṛ, *ṭ, *ṃ, *ḷ, *ṛ begins a word.[7] In the final position any consonant (probably except *ñ) can occur,[8] but all stops in the final position are followed by a fully predictable, therefore automatic (so-called enunciative, i.e. morphophonemic) *-u*, a kind of vocoid release.[9]

* My introduction to Dravidian morphology will consist of three parts: the first two parts deal with 'syntagmatic morphology' (Part One: Nouns and Adjectives, Part Two: Verbs and Indeclinables) while the third part deals with what may be called 'lexical morphology' or 'word-formation' (Part Three: Derivation and Composition). Parts Two and Three will be published at a later date.

CHART 1

DRAVIDIAN LANGUAGES

Name	Abbreviation	Localization	Number of speakers	Beginnings of literature
Tamil	Ta.	Tamilnadu (Madras State), parts of Ceylon, SE Asia, SE Africa	30,465,442 ± 4 mil.	3rd-2nd Cent. B.C.
Irula	Ir.	Nilgiri Mountains	4124	non-literary
Malayalam	Ma.	Kerala State, Madras City	16,994.919	13th Cent. A.D.
Kota	Ko.	Nilgiri Mountains	862	non-literary
Toda	To.	Nilgiri Mountains	765	non-literary
Badaga (a Ka. dialect?)	Bad.	Nilgiri Mountains	85,463	non-literary
Koḍagu	Koḍ.	Goorg (Kūrag)	78,202	non-literary
Kannaḍa	Ka.	Mysore State, cities of Madras and Madurai	17,415,827	9th Cent. A.D.
Tuḷu	Tu.	North Kerala, Southern Mysore	934,849	non-literary
Telugu	Te.	Andhra State, Madras City, SE Asia	37,642,439 ± 1 mil.	11th Cent. A.D.
Kolami	Kol.	Madhya Pradesh, Northern Andhra	46,065	non-literary
Naikṛi (Kol. dialect) (= *LSI*, Bhili of Basim)	Nk.	*ibid*.		non-literary
Naiki	NK.(Ch.)	Chanda distr. of Madhya Pradesh	ca. 1000	non-literary
Parji	Pa.	Bastar, Madhya Pradesh	84,607	non-literary
Koṇḍa (Kūbi)	Koṇḍ.	Viśakhapatnam and Śrīkākulam distr. of Andhra, Korāpuṭ distr., Orissa	12,298	non-literary
Gadba (Ollari)	Ga. (Oll.)	Korāpuṭ, Orissa	ca. 2000	non-literary
Gadba (Salur)	Ga. (S.)	Salur, Korāpuṭ, Orissa		non-literary
Gadba (Pottangi) (a Go. dialect?)	Ga. (P.)	Pottangi, Korāpuṭ, Orissa		non-literary
Dorli (a Go. dialect?)	Do.	South Bastar	35,455	non-literary
Koya (a Go. dialect?)		along river Godavari, Andhra Pradesh, Madhya Pradesh, Orissa	139,710	non-literary
Pengo	Pe.	Korāpuṭ, Orissa	1,254	non-literary

CHART 1 (Continued).

DRAVIDIAN LANGUAGES

Name	*Abbreviation*	*Localization*	*Number of speakers*	*Beginnings of liter.*
Maṇḍa	Manḍ.	Thuamul Rampur distr. , Kalahandi		non-literary
Kui (Khond)	Kui	Orissa	510,907	non-literary
Kuvi (Khond)	Kuvi	Orissa	168,027	non-literary
Gondi	Go.	Madhya Pradesh	ca. 2,000,000	non-literary
Kuru<u>kh</u>	Kur.	Bihar, Orissa, Madhya Pradesh	1,132,931	non-literary
Malto	Malt.	Bihar, West Bengal	88,645	non-literary
Brahui	Br.	Qalat, Hairpur, Hyderabad in W. Pakistan, South Afghanistan (?)	2 00,000 40,000 (?)	non-literary

NOTE: It is almost certain that a number of other Dravidian languages will be added to the list as research in the field proceeds. It seems that Kuṟumba (South Dravidian), Beḷa:ri (SDr), Koraga (South Dravidian?) and other languages will have to be added in the near future; the status of such languages as Poya, Savara, Yerukala, Burgaṇḍi, Kaikāḍī, Kāḍar etc. is quite uncertain.

0.4 As far as the *parts-of-speech system* is concerned the basic differentiation of the *noun* and the *verb* into separate form-classes raises no doubts since either has its own paradigm: nouns are inflected for case and number, and verbs for tense and person. The classification of *indeclinables* (which include both free and semi-free forms) as a distinct major form-class is based on their having no paradigm. Interjections (free) and onomatopoetic expressions (semi-free) may be classed with indeclinables as uninflected stems.[10] Criteria of syntactic behaviour fully agree with the classification based on morphology.

Such had probably been the situation in PDr. Later, however, new sub-classes of inflected stems emerged within the more general class of nouns: substantives and numerals, pronouns (a special sub-class of nouns since they are classified for person, and are marked for the feature 'inclusiveness' : 'exclusiveness') and adjectives (which are possibly genetically traceable to verbal and/or nominal roots); adjectives have neither nominal nor verbal paradigm, but a paradigm of their own in predication.[11] Finally, there exist in many Dr. languages the so-called echo-words which do not have an independent lexical meaning of their own and which have the same paradigm as the corresponding meaningful words.[12]

0.5 We shall proceed in this sketch according to the following scheme: 1. Nouns (1.1 Substantives proper, 1.2 Numeral substantives, 1.3 Pronouns). 2. Adjectives; 3. Verbs; 4. Indeclinables (4.1 Particles proper, 4.2 Interjections, 4.3 Adverbs, 4.4 Enclitics, 4.5 Onomatopoetic words, 4.6 Echo-words).

CHART 2

THE DRAVIDIAN PARTS-OF-SPEECH SYSTEM

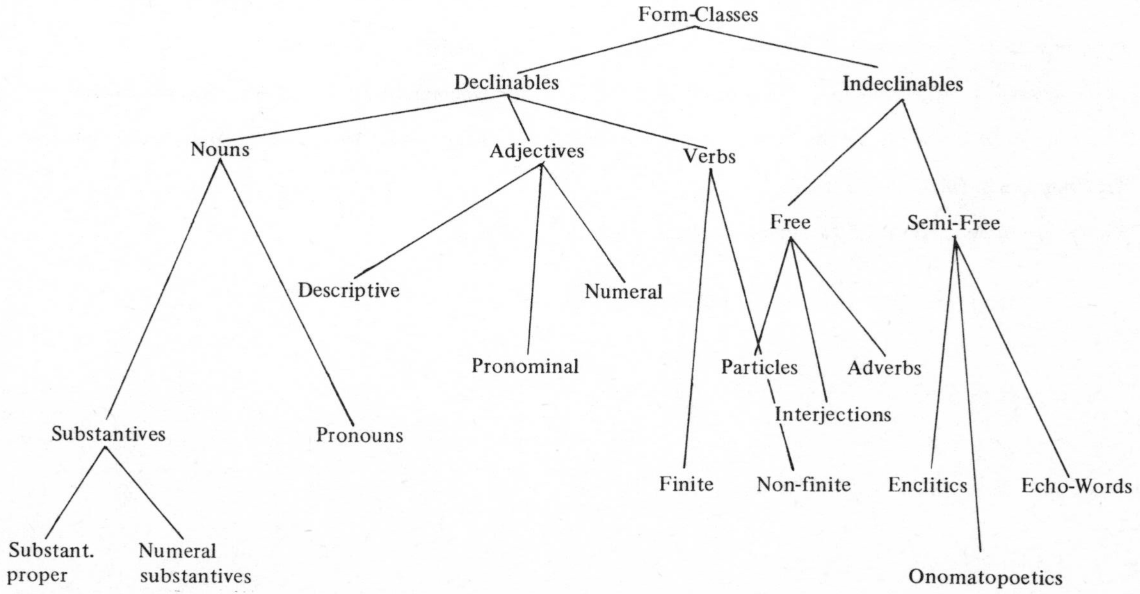

ILLUSTRATIONS

Subst. proper: *DED* 3288 Ta. *pal* 'tooth'

Numeral subst.: *DED* 834 [d] Ta. *o<u>n</u><u>r</u>u* 'one'

Pronouns: *DED* 4235 Ta. *yā<u>n</u>* 'I'

Descr. adjectives: *DED* 2265 Ta. *ce* 'straight'

Numeral adj. *DED* 834 [a] Ta. *oru* 'one'

Pronominal adj. *DED* 1 Ta. *a* 'that'

Finite verb forms: *DED* 1628 Ta. *cey-v-ē<u>n</u>* 'I (habitually) do, I shall do'

Non-finite verb forms: *DED* 1628 Ta. *cey-tu* 'doing, having done'

Particles: *DED* 351 [a] Ta. *itō* 'behold'

Adverbs: *DED* 351 [c] Ta. *i<u>n</u>i* 'hereafter'

Enclitics: Ta. *-um* 'and'

Onomatop.: *DED* 2628 Ta. *tiṭīr-* 'sudden(ly)'

Echo-words: Ta. [*paṇam*] - *kiṇam* 'some [money]'

1. NOUNS

Nouns in Dravidian are generally characterized by the presence of the categories of *gender* and *number, person* and *case*. Morphologically and syntactically, all nouns behave alike; substantives and the majority of pronouns show the category of gender, number and case; pronouns are a special subclass of nouns on account of an additional dimension : that of inclusiveness : exclusiveness; syntactically, they are substitutes. Numerals have the categories of gender and case, exceptionally of number; personal pronouns and personal nouns, the categories of gender, number, person and case.

1.1 SUBSTANTIVES

1.1.1 The gender of nouns in Dr. has a lexico-grammatical character. In many instances, the categories of gender and number are intermixed; thus e.g., in Koṇḍa, we have, apart from a common pl. suffix added both to masc. and non-masc. nouns, a special 'masculine plural' (*-r*); in Kol., we have a male sg. , male pl. , non-male sg. and non-male pl.

There are four major types of gender system in Dravidian: the SDr type, the CDr and NDr type, the Gondi Kui-Kuvi type, and the type with no gender differentiation.

1.1.1.1 In the majority *South Dravidian* languages (in Ta., Ma., Ka., Tu., Ko., Koḍ.; in Ko. and Koḍ., the 'non-person' form is undifferentiated for number), substantives are divided into two classes depending on their lexical meaning: one class contains substantives denoting human beings (Ta. *makkaḷ*) and, traditionally, divine beings (Ta. *teyvam*) and hermaphrodites (Ta. *pēṭi*), i.e. 'persons'; this class is termed, in Tamil, *uyartiṇai* 'the high class'; it is the personal class, the class of 'rational' beings; in Te. grammatical terminology, *mahat* comprises male persons in sg. and female persons in plural.

The other class contains substantives denoting animals, inanimate objects and abstract notions, i.e. 'non-persons'; this class is termed by Ta. grammarians *aḵṟiṇai* < *al-tiṇai*, lit. 'the non(-marked) class, the outside class', i.e. the class of ir-rational entities, of non-persons, in Te. *a-mahat* (comprising female persons and non-persons in sg., non-persons in pl.).

Within the 'rational' class, there is a further distinction based on natural sex between *masculine* and *feminine* substantives. In plural, the dichotomy runs differently: there is no distinction between masculine and feminine; there are only two genders – the epicene (male + female) and the neuter. The SDr situation may be thus characterised by the following scheme:

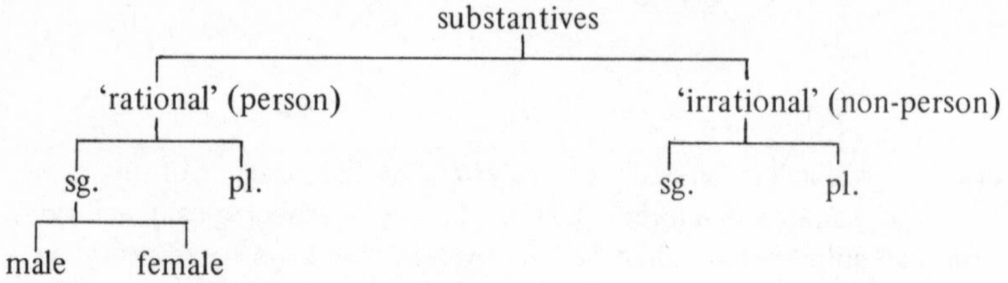

The grammatical gender of substantives is expressed through the concord with the corresponding forms of verbs and personal pronouns. The transfer of gender categories to verb-forms (and the agreement between substantives and personal pronouns) is the only channel of the expression of the gender-category in Dravidian.

The Old Ta. system of gender is outlined in *Tolk. Col.,* the initial rules of which deal with the *gender-number* category, and the morphemes which manifest it; these morphemes are, in the grammatical thinking of *Tolk.*, regarded clearly as cumuls: the marker *ṉ* manifests {sg. and masc.} , the marker *ḷ* {sg. and fem.} , the markers *r/pa/mār* manifest { pl. and masc. + fem.} , the markers *tu/ṟu/ṭu* manifest { sg. +non-person} and the markers *a/ā/va* manifest { pl. + non-person} . According to *sūtras* 1-9 of *Tolk. Col.*, there are thus two 'classes' (*tiṇai*, persons and non-persons) and five 'person-gender-number' categories (*pāl*: masc. sg., fem. sg., epicene pl., non-person sg. and non-person. pl).

1.1.1.2 In Telugu, Naiki, Gadba and some other CDr languages, and in Kuruk̲h̲ and Malto, there is no distinction between feminine and neuter in the singular: cf. Ga.Oll. *sēpal vadanḍ* 'the boy came' vs. *māl vada* 'the girl came': *kor vada* 'the fowl came'; *ī sēpal niyaṭonḍ* 'this boy is good' vs. *ī māl niyaṭe* 'this girl is good' : *ī kor niyaṭe* 'this fowl is good'. In these languages, the main dichotomy is masculine : non-masculine in the sg., and epicene (i.e. male + female) : neuter in the plural. However, e.g. in Ga.(Oll.), the male nouns generally take a different pl. suffix (*-r*), than female and neuter nouns (*-v, -l*), so that there is an overlap with the situation as outlined in 1.1.1.3.

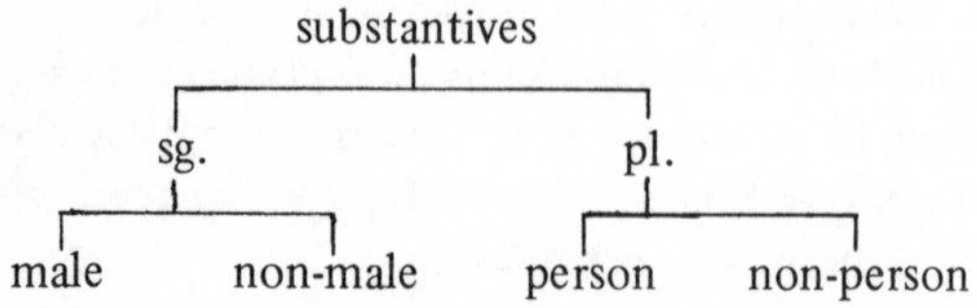

1.1.1.3 In Gondi, Koṇḍa, Kolami-Parji, but especially clearly in Kui-Kuvi, there are only two genders for both numbers – masculine versus non-masculine. Cf. Gondi *kāṇḍī* 'boy', pl. *kāṇḍīr : veylō* 'woman', pl. *veylōk,* just like *marā* 'tree', pl. *marāk.* Kui *āpo* 'son', pl. *āporu : mrau* 'daughter', pl. *mrauska,* just like *nāju* 'village', pl. *nāska.*

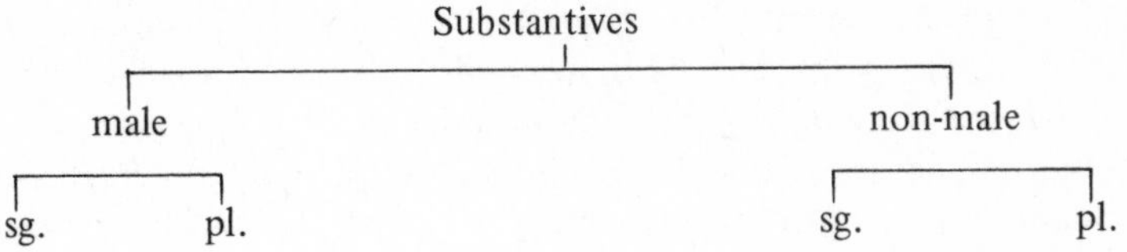

1.1.1.4 Brahui, Toda and Malayalam do not have the category of gender. These languages seem to have each lost the gender-category in their respective independent developments. However, as M. B. Emeneau makes me kindly aware (in personal communication), "gender and concord should perhaps be defined in such a way that the demonstrative 'gender'-distinctions of Malayalam can be treated as a gender-system. It is the lack even of this much that makes Toda and Brahui so peculiar".

1.1.1.5 The problem of the reconstruction of the situation in PDr has not yet been satisfactorily solved. Final opinion has not been expressed either whether PDr had the category of gender at all. It seems, however, that the situation as reflected by the *Kui-Kuvi* sub-family (plus Gondi Koṇḍa Kol. Pa.) may be considered as the preservation of the original state of affairs.[13] Caldwell's suggestion was that gender in Dr. is a later phenomenon, the origin of which is connected with the development of 'proniminal' suffixes in some loanwords, cf. Ta. *tēvu* 'deity' : *tēv-an̲* 'god', *tēv-i* 'goddess'.[14] However, the presence of gender with the substantives which do not possess 'pronominal' suffixes (i.e. when stem = root, like Ta. *āṇ* 'man' masc, *peṇ* 'woman' fem., *pal* 'tooth' neutr.) proves that the category of gender is not connected with derivation.[15]

According to J. Bloch and M.B. Emeneau, the basic binary division characteristic for Te., CDr and NDr (i.e. types 2 and 3), was also very probably characteristic for PDr.[16] Krishnamurti agrees with Bloch and Emeneau. The separation between the feminine and neuter genders seems to be later.[17]

T. Burrow and S. Bhattacharya, on the other hand, think that "the three gender system of Tamil-Kannada originally prevailed in the rest of Dravidian, and that the introduction of a two-gender system is an innovation of Telugu and the Central Dravidian languages".[18]

As far as Toda and Brahui is concerned, they have, as said above, lost all traces of the gender system, but while in Toda (cf. To. *aθ* 'he, she, it' <*atu) loss of gender took place without any stimulus from outside, it seems more than probable that in the case of Brahui Iranian influence (Balochi or Persian) can be postulated.[19]

Andronov takes no side in the issue.[20] We would, however, tend to agree with Bloch, Emeneau and Krishnamurti, and disagree with Burrow and Bhattacharya, though we realize that the wholeproblem has not been finally solved.

Arguing, though, purely from the facts of geographical distribution, it is the Telugu and Kurukh-Malto situation (i.e. masculine *versus* non-masculine in the sing., epicene *versus* neuter in the plural) which should be reconstructed for PDr, since Telugu is not geographically contiguous with Kur.-Malto, and since it does not share any other innovation with the two NDr languages. This argument was brought forward with force by P.S. Subrahmanyam (cf. ftn. 17).

Last but not least one should mention the fact that in all Dr. languages, gender distinctions are also expressed purely lexically with substantives, and this seems to have been the 'primitive' method; cf. Ta. *āṉ kuḻantai* 'male child, boy' : *peṇ kuḻantai* 'female child, girl'; Kui (Friend-Pereira) *mrēh' mīḍa* 'boy' : *āsa mīḍa* 'girl'.

1.1.2 There are two numbers in Dravidian – *singular* and *plural*. However, the overt morph of plural is not always obligatory. It is regular with the category of personal substantives, whereas with non-personal substantives, it does occur optionally (its occurrence or non-occurrence depending frequently on the context, or on the style).

1.1.2.1 The most frequently occurring plural suffix has the shape *-(*n*)*k*V*ḷ*(*u*) (where V = *a, i, u*).[21] The resulting phonemic shape is different in different languages (some lose the initial velar stop element, some lose the final element of the morph; there is also a number of morphophonemic variations).

LT: -(*k*)*kaḷ*, cf. *āṇ-kaḷ* 'men, males', *peṇ-kaḷ* 'woman', *malai-kaḷ* 'mountains', *ī-kkal* 'flies'.

CT: -(*k*)*ka*, cf. *pasu-kka* 'cows', *maran-ka* 'trees', *a:ṇ-ka* 'males', *janan-ka* 'people'. The LT shape of the pl. morpheme may obviously be considered as the underlying form *vis-à-vis* the CT shape.

Ma.: shows very close affinity with Ta. -(*k*)*kaḷ*, -(*ṅ*)*ṅal*, cf. *kuṭṭi-kaḷ* 'children', *paśu -kkaḷ* 'cows', *paṭaṅ-ṅaḷ* 'pictures'.

Ko.: -*gūḷ*,[22] cf. *kōv-gūḷ* 'the Kotas', *ton-gūḷ* 'the Todas', *marm-gūḷ* 'trees'.

In Ko. , number is not an obligatory category. The conditions for the appearance of this suffix have not yet been completely determined. It seems that pl. suffix is obligatory in inanimate nouns.

Ka.: *-gaḷ(u)*, cf. *hola-gaḷu* 'fields'. In coll. Ka., also *-gōḷu, -guḷu/-gḷu*, e.g. *nāygōḷu, nāyguḷu* 'dogs', *maniglu* 'houses';[23] irregular pl. *mak- (ka)ḷu* 'children' (W. Bright).

Koḍ.: **-ka(ḷ)*, cf. *aṇṇë* 'elder brother' : pl. *aṇṇaṅga, kōḍeṅga* 'monkeys', *pūneya* 'cats', *nayiya* 'dogs'.

Tu.: *-ḷu, -kuḷu,* cf. *tare-ḷu* 'heads', *pū-kuḷu* flowers', *pili-kḷu* 'tigers'.

Te.: *-lu, -kalu, -kulu/-galu, -gulu,* cf. *pilla-lu* 'children', *ennika-lu* 'elections', *illu* 'house' : pl. *iḷḷu; mrān-kulu* 'trees', *goḍu- gulu* 'umbrellas', OTe. *-ḷ(u), -l(u), -uḷ, -ul, -aḷ.*

Kol.: *-l, -ul : kaye-l* 'fish pl'., *kala-l* 'dreams', *toren-l*<? **tērensil* 'younger brothers', *āv-ul* 'fathoms'; *-kul : muḍi-kul* 'knots'; *-sil : zōḍ-sil* 'joints'.

Nk.: *-kuḷ, -ku/-gu : pal-kuḷ, pal-ku, pal-gu* 'teeth'; *-(u)l : kī-l* 'hand'; *-śil, -śikuḷ* <? **śilkuḷ : tōren-śil* 'brothers', *tōrnda-śikuḷ* 'sisters'.

Pa.: *-kul: pel-kul* 'teeth'; *-l, -ul/-il: maḍi-l* 'axes', *kerbe-l* (sg. *kerba*) 'eggs', *pēn-ul* 'lice', *nelň-il* 'moons, months' (sg. *neliň*); *-cil, -til: cavko-cil* 'pestles', *mā-cil* 'girls', *car-til* 'necks'.

Ga.: -V] *-l: ki-l* 'hands'; C] *-il/ul: eg-il* 'leaves', *amb-ul* 'arrows'; *-kil/-kul: sir-kil* 'buffaloes', *kaṇ-kul* 'eyes'; *-gil/-gul: kāl-gil* 'legs', *sir-gul* 'veins'; *-sil/-sul: var-sil* 'paddy-pl.', *keko-sul* 'ears'; *-til: kanīr-til* 'tears'.

It is clear that there is an isogloss uniting Kol. Nk. Pa. and Ga. with the following suffixes: **-(V)ḷ/*-kVḷ*, and **-cVḷ/*-tVḷ*, prob. < **-cVḷ*, where V = **i/u*, prob. < *i.

Go.: *-k* (and *-īk*); *-sk/-hk; -ṅg* (*-ṅ*): *kai-k* 'hands', *kor-k* (sg. *kor*) 'fowls'; *rō-hk* (sg. *rōn*) 'houses'; *mē-sk* (sg. *mēnj*) 'eggs'; *ḍuvvāl-īk* 'vultures'; *pittē-ṅg* 'birds' *versē-ṅ* 'squirrels'.

Koṇḍa: *-k(u); -g(u); sku; -ṅ (u)*: *komku* (sg. *komu*) 'horns'; *koṟh-ku* (sg. *koṟu*) 'hens'; *koṟonal-sku* (sg. *koṟonali*) 'nursing mothers'; *aye-k* (sg. *aya*) 'women'; *mēmar-gu* (sg. *mēmari*) 'husbands'; *ko'er-ṅu* 'sickles', *kurra-ṅ* 'male calves', *kome-ṅ* (sg. *koma*) 'branches'.

Kui: *-ka/-ga* for neuter pl.; *-ska/-saka* for fem.pl.; *-nga: sōr-ka* 'hills', *nās-ka* 'villages'; *kan-ga* 'eyes'; *ōḍa-nga* 'goats'; *aja-saka* 'mothers'; *angi-ska* 'younger sisters'.

Kuvi: *-ka; -ska; -nga; kūt-ka* 'mushrooms' (sg. *kūndū*); *kōska* 'fowls, hens' (sg. *koiyū*); *kōma-nga* 'branches'; *seppu-ṅa* 'shoes'.

It is quite clear that one isogloss unites Go. and Koṇḍa with the pl. suffixes **-k(V)* and **ṅ(V)* < **-nk(V)*, and a wider one including Gondi Koṇḍa Kui-Kuvi (as well as Pengo and Manḍa) with the markers of pl. **-k(V) and *-nk(V)*.

Kuru<u>kh</u> and Malto do not have etymologically related plural suffixes. In Kuru<u>kh</u>, substantives of the non-personal class, usually without a pl. morph, may be combined with *-guṭṭhī, -guṭhi, -guṭṭhi* (?) 'flock, multitude' to express (collective, or mass) plural, cf. *man-guṭhi* 'trees' (*LSI* 412), *k͟hess-guṭṭhī* 'paddy (of different kinds)' cf. also *ālī-guṭhi-ar* (*LSI* 412) 'wives'. For a remote possibility of a connection, cf. Pkt. *guṭṭha-* 'clump, clump of grass', Hi. *guṭhnā* 'to be knotted together', or Nahali *goṭhi* 'clan' (cf. Hi. *goṭh* 'assembly' or *goṭī* 'relation, kindred'.)[24]

Brahui: *-k* with the allomorphs *-āk, -g͟hāk* and *-g͟hāsk*, cf. *bā-k* 'mouths', *k͟hal-k* 'stones', *piḍ-ḍ-āk* 'stomachs', *parra-g͟hāk* 'wings', *lumma-g͟hāsk* 'mother and her people'.

The allomorphy of the non-male (or non-personal) plural marker entitles us to split the CDr group of languages into two subgroups: one Kolami-Parji, another Gondi – Kui-Kuvi, with Te. standing somewhat apart. In Te. the statistically absolutely predominant pl. marker of this type is *-lu* (according to Krishnamurti, *Telugu Verbal Bases,* 257-58, the pl. marker has to be reconstructed as PDr *-Vḷ "in over 99 percent of cases" for Telugu).

There seem to be at least two clear-cut isoglosses which may be based on the distribution of the pl. suffix of the non-personal substantives: one uniting Ta. Ma. Ko. Ka. and possibly Koḍ. with pl. *- *(n)kVḷ* where V = *a* in most cases; the other uniting Go. Koṇḍa, Kui-Kuvi and Brahui with pl. *-*(n)k (V)*. The third isogloss, not so clear, seems to unite Te. Kol. Nk. Pa. Ga. and possibly Tu. with pl. *-*(V)ḷ*/*-*kVḷ*. Hence we see that the PDr reconstruction of this suffix as *-*(n)kVḷ(u)* is founded on solid grounds. Though the details remain to be worked out, it is rather clear what happened: there was a number of splits; while, roughly speaking, SDr has preserved both the velar plosive element and the *ḷ-element of the original morph, Central and North Dravidian has preserved only the (prenasalised) velar stop element. Kuruk͟h and Malto lost the reflex of this suffix totally. Tu. and Te., with a closely related group of Kol. Nk. and Pa., have preserved rather the *-*ḷ*, and, alternatively, the *-*k* and *-*ḷ* elements, but the nasal element was lost in these languages.

1.1.2.2 According to J. Bloch, the reconstructed PDr suffix is, *au contraire*, a coalescent form of two plural suffixes, viz. *-*k(V)* and **Vḷ(u)*.[25] This hypothesis of Bloch is strongly supported by such forms as e.g. Nk. (Ch.) *kī* 'hand' : pl. *kī-l, kī-l-ku*[26] on the one hand, and, on the other hand, by the existence, in one and the same language, of pl. morphs which go back to *-*ḷ*, as e.g. Nk. *kī-l* 'hands', as well as to *-*k*, as e.g. Nk. *pal-ku* 'teeth'. Cf. also Burrow and Bhattacharya, *The Parji Language*, p. 12: "Clearly there were in early Dravidian two independent plural suffixes of the noun, *k* and *ḷ*, about whose original distribution it is not now possible to say anything." If we accept this hypothesis of a coalescent plural morph, then we may draw the following very tentative conclusion: from the existence of only the reflexes of *-*k* in North Dravidian (Brahui) and Gondi-Konda Kui-Kuvi, we may infer that *the velar stop* is preferably to be regarded as the earliest Dravidian suffix of substantive plurals of the non-personal class. Instead of a series of splits, we may then presuppose a series of mergers of this original (prenasalised?) velar occlusive with an *-ḷ element accompanied or unaccompanied by vowel.

According to Andronov, the suffixes with the velar stop (type -[*n*]*ka*) are secondary; they develop through the loss of the final -*ḷ* along the following line: -(*ⁿ*)*kVḷ*(*u*) : -(*n*)*kV* + *Vḷ*(*u*) > (*n*)*kVḷ*(*u*) > (*n*)*kV*.[27] What he says is definitely true about, e.g., colloquial Tamil, where the type -(*n*)*ka* is almost certainly a development from -(C)*kaḷ*. It may also be true about Koḍ. However, this represents a much later, almost 'historical' development.

1.1.2.3 As far as the usage of the pl. marker in the non-personal nouns is concerned: in SDr, the 'neuter' pl. marker is fully optional. Historically, it is almost totally absent from the earliest strata of Tamil literary texts (about 9 instances). In Ma., Ko., Ka., Koḍ. and Tu., its use is optional, dependant upon context and style, as in modern Ta. In NDr, Kur. and Malt. do not have any pl. suffix for neuter nouns, in Br. its use is optional, depending on the context. Since the absence or the optional, even rare use of the neuter pl. marker is a feature common to SDr and NDr as well as to Old Ta., it should be attributed to PDr. In CDr, however, the pl. marker is 'a very essential category', and its regular use can be considered as innovation of CDr.[28]

1.1.2.4 Another plural morph of Dr. is the suffix *-(V)*r*. Its occurrence is limited to the nouns of the personal class and to pronouns (of the 'person' class).

Ta.: *avaṉ* 'that man' : *avar* 'those people'; OTa. *makaḷ-ir* 'girls, women', *peṇṭ-ir* 'women', *kēḷir* 'relatives'; *vēḷir* 'name of a clan' (all after retroflexes), cf. Iruḷa *poṇḍiru* 'id'..
Ma.: *īḻavar* 'toddy-drawers', *avar* 'those persons'.
Ko. *avn* 'that man': *avr* 'those persons'.
Ka.: *ava* 'that man': *avar* 'those persons'; *arasar* 'kings', *striyar* 'women', *tandeyar* 'fathers'; *appandiru* 'fathers'.
Coll. Ka.: *magdiru* 'sons', *huḍgru, huḍru* 'boys'.
Tu.: *āye* 'that man' : *āru̥* 'those persons'.
Te.: *vā̆ḍu* 'that man' : *vāru* 'those persons'; *allŭḍu* 'son-in-law' : pl. *alluṇḍru, alluru; dēvaru* 'gods', *rāyaru* 'kings', *meyyuru* 'friends', *pagaRu* <**paganRu* 'enemies'.
Kol.: *am* 'that man' : *avr* 'those men'; *kōlavan* 'Kolam man' : pl. *kōlavar; mās* 'man' : pl. *māsur; budiak-er* 'old men', *vēduker* 'physicians' (*-er* after *k*).
Nk.: *avnd* 'that man' : *avr* 'those men'.
Pa.: *ōd* 'that man' : *ōr* 'those men'; *muttaker* 'oḷd men', *kummaler* 'potters'; *tāter* 'fathers', *parjer* 'Parjas', *toled* 'brother' : pl. *toler*.
Ga.: *ōnḍ* 'that man' : *ōr* 'those men'; *muttakor* 'old men', *amabar* 'our fathers',

ilenḍ bridegroom' : pl. *iler*.

Go.: *kāṇḍī-r* 'boys', *tōṇḍa-r* 'male friends'; *kall-īr* 'thieves', *tott-ūr* 'ancestors'; *māmūriāl-ōr* 'fathers-in-law', *dādāl-ōr* 'fathers', *vertālōr* 'guests', *aṛjalōr* 'bears'.

Koṇḍa: *vāṉṟu* 'that man' : *vār* 'those man'; *tōṇḍa* 'male friend' : pl. *tōṇḍar.*

Kui: *aanju* 'that man' : *aaru* 'those man'; *ābaru* 'fathers', *āporu* 'sons', *tanji* 'fathers' : pl. *tanjeru.*

Kur.: *ās* 'that man' : *ār/abṛar* 'those persons'; *ālar* 'men', *mukkar* 'woman', *ālī-guṭhi-ar* 'wives'.

Malt.: *āh* 'that man' : *ār* 'those persons'; *maleh* 'a man' : pl. *maler, malniṯẖ* 'a woman' : pl. *malnīr, peli* 'a woman' : pl. *peler; taṅgad bagter* 'son-many', 'sons' (*LSI* 448).

Br. does not have the reflex of *-(V)*r*. It has only the velar plosive for all substantives: *īṛ-k* 'sisters', *māk* 'sons', *amīk, amīrāk* 'chieftains', *arē* 'person' : pl. *arisk.*

1.1.2.5 In some languages, the suffix -(V)*r* combines with some of the shapes of the suffix -(*n*)*k Vḷ*(*u*), forming thus a new coalescent pl. suffix: cf. Ta. *avar-kaḷ* 'those persons', *aracarkaḷ* 'kings', Ka. (coll.) *hudgrgaḷu* 'boys', (lit.) *mahāś-yarugaḷu* 'gentlemen', OKa. *goravarkkaḷ* 'masters, gurus', OTe. *raguṟla* 'of the kings', Nk. (Ch.) *tōlen* 'brother', pl. *tōlen-ku-r,* Go. *kallē-r-k* 'thieves', *tammurk* 'brothers'.

Two points should be mentioned in this connection: First, considering cases like Nk. (Ch.) *tōlen-ku-r* 'brothers' (cf. the structurally analogous Kur. *ālī-guṭhi-ar* 'wives'), where the linear order of the suffixes is not *-*r* + *-*k* but the reverse, it seems that at the time of the beginning of this particular trend, the plural morphs were rather 'free' and independent. Second, since the tendency to combine the two plural morphs (**r* +*-*k*) may be found not only in SDr but also in such languages as Go. or Nk., it seems that the trend must have started as far back as (prob.) the later stages of PDr itself.

1.1.2.6 Another pl. suffix is *-*m*; it is limited mostly only to the 1. and 2. p. pl. pronouns. Cf. the following instances:

1.p.sg.	Ta. *yāṉ, nāṉ*	pl. *yām, nām*
	Ma. *ñān*	**ñām-kaḷ>ñāṅṅaḷ*
	Ko. *ān*	*ām*
	To. *ōn; aθ* 'he, she, it'	*ām* (excl.)/*ōm* (incl.); *aθām* 'those persons or things'
	Ka. *ān, nān*	*ām*
	Kod. *nānī, nā*	*eŋga, naŋga* (< **em*-, **nam*-)
	Tu. *yānu, yēnu, yānụ, ēnụ*	*eṅkuḷụ* (< **em*-)
	Te. *ēnu, nēnu*	*ēmu, nēmu, mēmu*

Kol. *ān*	*ām*
Nk. *ān*	*ām*
Nk. (Ch.) *ān*	*ām(e)*
Pa. *ān*	*ām*
Ga. *ān*	*ām*
Go. *anā, nanā*	*ammaṭ, mamāṭ* etc.
Koṇḍa *nān*	*mān; māp(u)* (excl.), *māṭ (u)* (incl.)
Pe. *ān/āne*	
Manḍ. *ān*	
Kui *ānu, nānu*	*āmu, māmu*
Kuvi *nānu, nānū*	*māmbu, māmbū*
Kur. *ēn*	*ēm*
Malt. *ēn*	*ēm*
Br. *ī*	

The pl. marker *-*m*, occurring originally in the pronouns in contrast to the sg. *-*n*, occurs as the pl. suffix in the imperative in Old Ta. (cf. the suffixes *-m-ō, -m-iyā* and *iku-m* in forms like *ceṉmō* 'will you go! '), in Kota (cf. Emeneau, *Kota Texts*. 57, forms like *tinm* 'eat [pl.]!', *ibid*. 38), Old Kannada, and the Brahui imperative pl. suff. *-bo* (cf. forms like *tik̲h̲-bo* 'place, put', *bim-bo* 'hear') may also be derived from this pl. marker *-*m*. It is tempting to connect the regular To. pl. marker *-ām*, cf. *mox-ām* 'boys', *kūx-ām* 'girls', *pūf-ām* 'flowers', *aθ-ām* 'they'.

1.1.2.7 There is yet another pl. morph, occurring with substantives and pronouns alike, viz. *-(V)*v*. This suffix, too, is rather widespread throughout the family, its occurrence mostly (but not entirely) restricted to the non-personal class. With pronouns, cf. Ta. *av/avai* 'those things', Ma. *ava* 'id.', Ka. *avu* 'id.', Tu. *avu* 'id.', Te. *avi* 'id.', Kol. *adav* 'those women or things', Nk. *adav* 'id.', Go. Koi. *au* 'id'. , Kui *avi* 'id.', Br. *dād* 'this person or thing' :pl. *dāfk*,i.e. Br. *-ād* : * **at-*, Br. *-āf-* : **av-*, Br. *ē, ēd* 'that' : pl. *ēfk*. With substantives, cf. Kol. *aliak-ev* 'male buffaloes', *appakev* 'father's sisters', *ammanev* 'mothers', Pa. *tal-l-ov* 'mothers', (Southern Pa.) *bay-ev* 'elder sisters'.[30]

The Brahui situation is curious. First, there is total absence of gender category (possibly, but not surely under the impact of neighbouring Iranian languages); second (and this is connected with the absence of gender, obviously) Br. has no reflex of the 'higher' class pl. marker *-(V)*r*; in fact, it has the reflexes of only two pl. markers, *-*k* and *-*v*. This gives us pause: is not, after all, the Brahui situation (i.e. no gender, and one pl. marker, *-*k,* for all substantives, another, *-*v*, for pronouns) a preservation of the original, pre- or proto-Dravidian state of affairs?

1.1.2.8 In conclusion we may sum up the situation as follows: We have obviously to reconstruct, for PDr, or at least for its later stages, the following plural suffixes: (1) *-(*n*)*kVḷ*(*u*), which may be either considered as a coalescent suffix of the earlier *-*k*(V) and *-*Vḷ*(*u*), or as one suffix with a number of subsequent splits (this is more probable,since *-*k* and *-*kaḷ* are in complementary distribution in terms of geographical situation): (2) *-(V)*r*, limited to the nouns of the personal class and to pronouns of the 'person' (male, or male + female) class; *-*m*, limited, with some exceptions (? Toda) to the pers. pronouns of the 1. and 2. persons; *-(V)*v*, occurring with substantives, and with pronouns of the 'non-person' (neuter) class. It is also suggested here (not even as a hypothesis, but as a mere suggestion) that, for the early stages of PDr and for pre-Dr., we might probably reconstruct a **-*k* as a pl. suffix for substantives irrespective of gender distinctions, **-*m* as a pl. suffix of personal pronouns (in contrast to **-*n*), and **-*v* as another pl. suffix of pronouns (demonstrative pronouns) transferred in some languages to substantives.

1.1.3 Substantives are declined for case by means of case-suffixes appended either to the stem (unexpanded or expanded) or to the nominative form. The stem remains phonemically unchanged while declined, and the case-markers, too, are easily identifiable, since only relatively few and unimportant morphophonemic changes occur at the boundary between stem (or nominative form) and the inflexional suffixes. Case-suffixes are almost always identical for sg. and pl. Ka. *kāl* 'leg', abl. sg. *kāl-inda* 'from the leg' : pl. *kālugaḷ-inda* 'from the legs'.

1.1.3.1 A characteristic feature of Dravidian noun-inflection is *the expansion of some stems by empty morphs.*[31] Thus e.g. in Ta. substantives and pronouns are extended by *-iṉ-*/*-aṉ-* or *-tt*/*u*, cf. Ta. *maram* 'tree' (nom.), *mara-* (stem) : *mara-ttu-kku* (dat.) 'to the tree'; *atu* 'that thing', *at-aṯ-ku* (< *at-aṉ-ku*) 'to that thing' (dat.). In Ka., masc. and fem. nouns with final *-a*, and neuters with final *-a*, have extended stems with an added *-n* and *-d* respectively, cf. *huḍuga-* 'boy' : *huḍugan-* (extended stem) : *huḍugan-inda* 'from the boy'; *mara-d-inda*, (coll.) *mar-d-inda* 'from the tree'; nouns ending in *-u* or consonants sometimes extend their stems by *-in*, cf. *guru* 'teacher' : *guru-v-in-inda* 'from the teacher'. The empty morphs occurring most frequently have the following phonemic shapes: *-t-*, *-d-*, *-tt-*, *-n-*, *-an-*/*-in-*, *-u-*. A good and well-documented inventory of empty morphs in the comparative perspective may be found in S.V. Shanmugam's "Inflectional Increments in Dravidian" (*DL* [1969], 23-58). According to Shanmugam, it is necessary to reconstruct, for PDr.,the following empty morphs: *-*an-*, *-*ṯṯ-*, *-*in-*, *-*a-*, *-*tt-*. In some languages, combinations of these morphs occur, too. *-*an-* occurs after demonstr./interrog. neuter sg. pronouns (PDr. **itu* : **it-an-*). *-*ṯṯ-* occurs after demonstr./interrog. neuter pl. pronouns (PDr. **avay* : **avatt-*). *-*in-*occurs after vowel-endings and after all consonantal endings except *-m* and *-n.* **-a-* can be reconstructed in the pers. pronouns before dative. **-tt-* occurs with the **-m/*-n* ending in the genitive (PDr **maram/ *maran* : **maratt-*).

The sequence of morphemes in an inflected form is

Root ± deriv. ± empty ± case

(Root ± deriv. = stem; stem ± empty = Expanded stem)

Examples:

Ta. R: *peṇ-* ± deriv. : O ± empty : O ± case: acc > *peṇṇai* 'woman'
R: *mar-* ± deriv. : *-a-* ± empty : *-tt-* ± case: acc. > *marattai* 'tree'
Ka. R. *man-* ± deriv. : *-e-* ± empty : O ± case: loc. > *maneyalli* 'in the house'
R: *mar-* ± deriv. : *-a-* ± empty: : *-d-* ± case: abl. > *maradinda* 'from the tree'

The plural marker *always* precedes case-suffixes, e.g. Ta. *maraṅ-kaḷ-ai* pl. accus. 'trees', Ka. *mane-gaḷ-inda* pl. abl. 'from the houses', Kur. *mukka-r-gē (LSI)* pl. dat. 'to the woman'. The case-markers in the plural are suffixed as a rule to the nominative form.

1.1.3.2 The number of cases is different in different languages; or, rather, is given differently by various authors describing the respective languages. Generally, no one of the languages lacks, in addition to the *nominative* or *subject-case*, an *accusative* or *direct object-case*, a *dative* or *indirect object-case*, a *genitive* or case of *adnominal relation* (with a 'possessive' sometimes distinguished), and, further, a case or cases which express some kind(s) of relation(s) in *space* and *time,* static or dynamic; finally, a case of *instrument,* and, sometimes, a case of *association.*

According to the native grammarians of Ta., Ma., Ka. and Te., there are eight cases, viz., nominative, accusative, instrumental, dative, ablative, genitive, locative, and vocative. *Tolk.*, the most ancient and independent of native 'Dravidian' grammars, denotes the cases as follows: *peyar* (lit. 'noun') = nom., *-ai* = acc., *-oṭu* = instr., *-ku* = dat., *-iṉ* = abl., *-atu* = gen., *-kaṇ* = loc., and *viḷi* (lit. 'summon') = voc. (*Tolk. Col.* 65).

As illustration, paradigms, from Ka. (SDr), Te., Kol., Pa., Kui (CDr), Kur., Malt. and Br. (NDr) are given next. Then, the suffixes will be tabulated, discussed and compared and, finally, a reconstruction attempted.

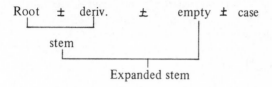

Kannaḍa

Nom.: *huḍ(u)ga* 'boy', *huḍ(u)gi* 'girl', *mara* 'tree' Acc.: *mara-v-annu* 'tree', *kāl-anna, kāl-na, kāl* 'leg' Instr.-Abl.: *kāl-inda, kāl-ininda, kāl-āginda* 'from the leg', *mane-y-inda, manāeginda* 'from the house' Dat.: *mar-ke, mara-kke* 'to the tree', *ḥuḍgan(i)ge* 'to the boy', *kāl-ge* 'to the leg' Gen.: *-a,*-A (morphophon. alter.): *huḍugan-a, huḍugn-a* 'of the boy, the boy's', *huḍigiy-a, huḍgī* 'of the girl, the girl's.' Loc.: *mane-y-alli, manē-li, man(e)-li, manāege* 'at (in) the house', *pāda-d-alli, pāddāge* 'at the foot'.[32]

Telugu

Nom.: *rāmuḍu* 'Rama', *pilla* 'girl', *gurramu* 'horse', Acc.: *śarma-nu* 'Sarma', *pilla-ni* 'girl' Instr.: *rāṭa, rā-ta* 'with a stone, by a stone', *mā-cāēta* 'by us' Dat.: *haydarābādu-ku* 'to Hyderabad', *ūri-ki* 'to town' Gen.: *rāmu-n-i* 'of Rama', *snēhituḍ-i* 'friend's', *iṇṭ-i* 'of the house'; *gurramu* 'of the horse', *rāmu-l-a* 'of Ramas' (pl.) Loc.: *bhāṣa-lō* 'in language', *iṇṭi-lō* 'in the house', *ūḷḷō* 'in town', *haydarābādulō* 'in H.' Soc.: *snēhituḍ-i-tōḍu* 'with friend', *sarōjā-tō* 'with S.'

Kolami

Nom.: *ella* 'house', *ūr* 'village' Acc.: *ella-n* 'house', *ūr-un* 'village' Dat.: *ella-ŋ* 'to the house', *ūr-uŋ* 'to the village' Loc. sg.: *ella-t* 'in, into, onto the house', pl.: *gurral-eŋ* 'onto the horses' sg.: *pilla-nadaŋ* 'to the woman', *patlak-naŋ* 'to the headman'; pl. *-adaŋ* Instr.: *tupuk-aḍ* 'with a gun', *kī-naḍ* 'with the hand' Abl.: *ūr-tanaṭ* from the village'

Parji

Nom.: *gōli* 'jackal', *mokom* face' Acc.: *gōli-n* 'jackal', *mokom-in* 'face' Dat.: (North) *ēnu-g* 'to the elephant', *pāp-ug* 'to the child' (South) *enu-ŋ* 'to the elephant', *pāp-uŋ* 'to the child' Gen.: *tāte-n* 'of the father', *bām-in* 'of the snake', *muṭṭe-t* 'of the pot', *mer-to* 'of the tree' Instr.: *gēri-noḍ* 'with the nail', *cavkol-oḍ* 'with the pestle' Loc.-Abl.: *kēti-t-i* (> *kētti*) 'in the winnowing basket', *polub-ti* 'in the village', *mer-ti* 'from the tree', *polb-el* 'in the village', *vāya-t-el* 'in the fields'

Kui

Nom.: *āba* 'father'	*mṛehenju* 'man'	*aja* 'mother'	*kōru* 'buffalo'
Acc.: *āba-i*	*mṛehen-i-i*	*aja-ni-i*	*kōru-tin-i*
Dat.: *āba-ki*	*mṛehen-i-ki*	*aja-n-gi*	*kōru-tin-gi*
Assoc.: *āba-ke*	*mṛehen-i-ke*	*aja-n-ge*	*kōru-tin-ge*
Abl.: *āba* + postp.	*mṛehen-i* + postp.	*aja-ni* + p.	*kōru* + postp.
Gen.: *āba*	*mṛehen-i*	*aja-ni*	*kōru*

Obl.: *āba-*   *mṛehen-i-*   *aja-n-(-i-)*   *kōru-(-t-in-)*

Kuruḵẖ

Nom.: *kukkos* 'boy'	*mukkā* 'woman'
Acc.: *kukkos-in*	*mukka-n*
Dat.: *kukkos-gē*	*mukka-gē*
Instr.: *kukkos-tī*	*mukka-n-tī*
Loc.: *kukkos-nū*	*mukkā-nū*
Gen.: *kukkos-gahi*	*mukkā-gahi*

Malto

Nom.: *maleh* 'man'
Acc.: *male-n*
Dat.: *male-k*
Instr.: *male-t*
Loc.: *male-no*
Abl.: *male-nte*
Gen.: *male-ki*

Brahui

Nom.: *ḵẖarās* 'bull'
Acc.: *ḵẖarās-e*
Dat.: *ḵẖaṛās-e*
Instr.: *ḵẖarās-aṭ*
Gen.: *ḵẖarās-nā*
loc.: *ḵẖarās-a ṭī* 'in the bull';
ḵẖarās-āi 'on, towards the bull'
Abl.: *ḵẖarās-ān*
Conj.: *ḵẖarās-to*

1.1.3.3 Two facts are particularly worth discussing with regard to the declension of substantives in Dravidian: first, the fact that some of the *empty morphs* have undoubtedly preserved, in many of the languages, *a grammatically relevant function*; second that, obviously, most of the *inflexional suffixes* had originally been *independent words*, and this independence is still frequently manifested in variou ways. In principal, a distinction is still discernible between "terminations with grammatical value" and "terminations with concrete value";[33] or, an even more detailed distinction can be made among case-suffixes with purely grammatical function, like e.g. the dative *-(*k*)*k*(*V*) ['indirect object'], terminations with the 'concrete value' still partly preserved like e.g. the comitative (sociative)*= *ōṭ/u,*

**-oṭan* (Ta. *-oṭu/-ōtu, -uṭa̲n*, Ma. *-oṭu/-oṭu*, Ko.*-ōṛ*, To. *wīṛ*, Ka. *oḍan, oḍam, oḍa* 'with', Tu. *oḍa* 'with', Te. *oḍam-*, *DED* 798), and postpositions which still behave as free forms, like Ta. *-koṇṭu* 'with' :*koṇṭu* 'having' taken', an adverb. participle (<*koḷ*) functioning as such in the language; or Ta. *-mēl* 'above' :*mēl* n. 'that which is over, surface, sky etc.' (*DED* 4173). In this way, we have so to speak, at present, three levels of grammatical abstraction, represented by the Dravidian case-terminations (the entire problem is of course nothing specific for Dravidian and is relevant to general linguistics; but this is the way how Dravidian has 'solved', until now, the problem of expressing 'case' relationships):

(3)	accusative suffix, dative suffix, genitive suffix	most highly 'grammaticalized' suffixes
(2)	terminations expressing comitative (sociative), locative and ablative relationships	less 'grammaticalized' terminations
(1)	postpositions occurring in functions expressing relationships in space (static/dynamic) and time; other postpositions derived from free noun and verb forms	least 'grammaticalized' postpositions

These different degrees of grammatical abstraction are manifested by morpho-syntactic 'freedom', and by the possibility to find etymological connections: on level (1), the degree of morpho-syntactic freedom is the greatest, and it is always possible to find a satisfactory etymological connection between a 'case-termination' and a free noun or verb form. On level (3), the markers of case-relationships are practically 'fused' with the unexpanded or expanded stems (i.e., no degree of morpho-syntactic 'freedom'), and it is in fact impossible to find a plausible etymological connection for any of them.

This whole discussion is valid on the historical and comparative plane (while, of course, in a strictly functional, synchronic description such pairs as Ta. *mēl*$_1$ subst. 'sky, etc.' and *-mēl*$_2$ postp. 'above' must be kept apart and separate). While it is possible to compare profitably such suffixes as the dative, the accusative, and to some extent, the genitive morphs in almost all the languages of the entire family and reach certain conclusions as to their etymological connection and the possibility of a reconstruction of the proto-forms of these suffixes, it becomes rather difficult once we get on to the instrumental and comitative suffixes, and almost impossible with regard to the terminations with 'concrete value' where similarities in phonemic shape and grammatical function are usually limited only to closely related or geographically contiguous languages.

Conclusion: With a fair amount of certainty, we can trace down, to a common phonemic shape and a common grammatical function, the dative, the accusative, perhaps the genitive, and the obliques in *-*t*- and *-V*n*. The most easily reconstructable, and the most widely spread throughout the whole family is the dative suffix, which may be reconstructed for PDr fairly safely as *-*(k)k (V)*[34].

On the level of purely synchronic and functional description, however, all this is of no relevance. In fact, we may posite an 'infinite' number of 'cases' for perhaps any Dr. language once we depart from the familiar types of paradigms forced upon us by traditional indigenous and European grammars especially of the literary languages. It is, for instance, sheer convention based on Tamil grammatical tradition (influenced no doubt by Sanskrit) that, as a rule, the number of cases given in Tamil is eight.[35] The paradigms of our current Dr. grammars, "modelled on the Sanskrit system reinforced by Latin" (Bloch: "modelés sur la grammaire sanskrite renforcée de la latine", *SGD* 16) are indeed misleading. Bloch is most probably right when he advocates only one fundamental flexion: that of the *oblique case* ("casoblique") marked or unmarked in relation to the *nominative case.* However, before we subscribe to this hypothesis of Bloch, let us examine the postulates: the oblique case and its functions; the grammatical relevance of some 'empty morphs'; the relative independence of inflexional elements; and whether a marker of the nominative can be traced.

1.1.3.3.1 It is a fact which can be recognized even in a rather superficial observation, that the *oblique stem* formed in most languages from the simple stem (i.e. root ±derivational suffix[es]) by a *-*t*- type or a *-*Vn*- type suffix, has a "more concrete value", "more definite meanings" (*des sens plus définis*, J. Bloch, *SGD* 12), in short, that it is a case which occurs as marker of *local, temporal,* or at least *adnominal* relations. With increasing time-depth, this function of the oblique stem, its 'concreteness', seems to be more pronounced. It is therefore quite clear that the morphs constituting this form, though they are classified traditionally with the 'empty morphs', have had, and have preserved, a grammatically relevant function. Cf. (a) in Old Tamil: -*tt/u* has almost always a 'grammatical meaning'; it occurs as marker of local and adnominal relations, and only very rarely as a suffix which derives an oblique stem simply and purely.[36] Cf. e.g., the following instances from a very old Ta. text (*Kuṟuntokai* 8.1): *māttu . . . uku . . . tīmpaḻam* 'sweet fruit, falling *from* the mango tree'. The other OTa oblique morph -*iṉ* is, with nouns, the marker of adnominal, locational and temporal relations; also the marker of comparison (cf. *Kuṟaḷ* 54.1 *peṇṇiṉ* 'in comparison with woman'); with verb nouns the marker of causal nexus.[37] (b) As far as CDr is concerned we may quote as illustrations the situation in Pa., Go. and Kui. In Parji, the case suffix -*t* or -*to* (South -*ta*) as a suffix of adnominal relation (e.g. *geṛet lōg* 'the people of the town', *muṭṭet nīr* 'the water of the pot', *polubto pelac* 'village priest'); but it also frequently has 'a local sense', cf. *edromta pinda* 'the fly on (his) chest', *ā gappet perkul* 'the rice in the basket'. The same -*t*- appears as a component of Pa. locative suffix *-t-i*, cf. *īpolubti* 'in this village'; cf. also Kol.-Naikṛi *-t* as the locative suffix: *ūrut* 'in the village'. That this is the oblique stem marker is clear from the fact that derivatives in Pa. are formed from this extended stem: *polub* (*DED* 3529) 'village', obl. *polubt-*, pronominalized (personal) noun *polubted* 'he-villager', *polubter* 'they-villagers' : *polubten* 'I-villager'. The identical *-t-* occurs elsewhere, too e.g. before an ablative suffix, e.g. *ān*[1] *kond-t-ar*[2] *iṛiyaten*[3] 'I[1] descended[3] from the mountain[2]'. The other oblique morph *-n* (*-in*), apart from having a genitive function, occurs, too, as 'augment'(empty morph) with ablative suffixes: *ḍuv-in-arre bāced* 'he escaped from the tiger'. For the Gondi situation, one may quote Bloch (*SGD* 11), who says: "Le thème ainsi défini, soit *paddī-t-*, *rō-t-*, est en réalité une forme à valeur de régime, formant groupe avec des postpositions . . . il en est même pour -n des noms supérieurs . . . Tout se passe donc comme si l'on avait deux types de déclinaison à deux cas, cas sujet et cas régime . . . " In other words, there are, again, two oblique stems, one in *-t-*, another in *-n-*, cf. *maṛsāl* 'man', obq. *maṛsān-*, and *chauvā* 'child', obq. *chauvāt-*, *rōn* 'house', obq. *rōt-*. The oblique base is, at least in some dialects and with some stems, identical with the dative-accusative case.

In Kui we again encounter the two morphs of the oblique, *-t-* and *-in-*, cf. *kōru* 'buffalo', accus. *kōru-t-in-i*. In the derived nouns, the oblique-genitive is said to be formed by *-i*, *-ni* (masc.-fem.) or *-a* (inferior gender). And, again, these "inflexional increments" (Winfield) may have simultaneously the function of genitive and accusative. I would rather, however, segment such forms as *neganju* 'good man' : *negari* 'good woman or thing' as *neg-an-ju* and *neg-ar-i* (cf. *neg-i* adj. 'good', *DED* 3096), and the obliques as *neg-an-i*, *neg-ar-in-i*, *neg-ar-a*, showing, as obl. suffixes, the ubiquitous Dr. oblique formative ("empty morph") **-Vn-*, realized in Kui as *-an/-in-*, cf. such accus. as *kōrutini* 'buffalo': segment *kōru-t-in-i*, i.e. 'stem- $empty_1$ - $empty_2$-accus.'. (c) For NDr, let us examine the situation in Brahui.Again, there appear the two omnipresent oblique stem formatives **-t-* and **-(V)n-*. The distribution is however different: the **-(V)n-* morph occurs only as a part of the genitive suffix: *k̲h̲arās-n-ā* 'of the bull', *bā-an-ā* 'of the mouth', *mār-an-ā* 'of the son' (and the *-V- reappears as 'incremental *-a-*' in other cases: *mār-a-to* 'with the son'). The **-t-*, on the other hand, occurs throughout the plural declension: *k̲h̲arās-k* 'bulls' nom.: *k̲h̲arās-t-ā* gen., *k̲h̲arās-t-e* dat.-accus., *k̲h̲arās-t-e-to* conj., etc.

1.1.3.3.2 The relative independence of inflectional elements in Dr. can best be discussed on the comparative and historical plane. With some of the postpositional elements this is unnecessary since the independent status is almost self-evident; as pointed out above, some of the postpositions, especially those used as markers of locational relations, still occur as free forms, as independent lexical items: e.g. Ta. *mēl* 'that which is over or above; sky; west; superiority, etc.' (*DED* 4173) : *-mēl* postp. 'on; above', e.g.: *mēcai mēl* 'on the table';

mēcaikku mēl 'above the table'; or Ga. (Oll.) *-tanḍrel* 'in, inside' : *ōnḍ*[1] *kuy*[2] *tanḍrel*[3] *īliṅinonḍ*[4] 'he[1] was falling[4] in[3] the well[2]'; or Kui *-nēḍe* 'on the ground, underneath': *nēḍe* (*DED* 2374) 'ground';*-senḍo* 'above, in the sky': *-senḍo-ki* 'to above', *-senḍo-ṭi* 'from above'. A comparative approach yields the recognition of the original independent status of such case-terminations as the Ta. suffix of sociative *-oṭu/-ōṭu, -uṭaṉ* (cf. *DED* 798 which shows that, originally, this has been a noun with the meaning 'union, togetherness', cf. Ka. *oḍan, oḍam, oḍa* 'union', and the use of this noun as qualifier preceding the head-noun in Ta., Ma., Ka., Tu., and Te.) < **-oṭ/u, *oṭ/a*; or of the Ta. Ma. Ka. Ko. *-uḷ,* To. *uṭ,* Te. *-lō*, which is widespread throughout the Dr. family as a substantive with the meaning of 'interior of a place; heart, mind; house' (cf. *DED* 600) < **-uḷ/ *-uḷ-V* or the Pa. *-kan/-ka,* a locative suffix (e.g. *an*[1] *kan*[2] *peru*[3] *vercil*[4] *cila*[5] 'there is not[5] much[3] rice[4] with[2] me[1]') which is undoubtly connected with Ta. *-kaṇ,* locative suffix current especially in OTa., cf. *Tirukkuṟaḷ* 52.1. *illāḷ kaṇ* 'in the mistress of the house'.[38] This suffix may be etymologized either as connected with *DED* 975 Ta. *kaṇ* 'place, site', Ka. *kaṇi* 'a place', or, in agreement with Bloch, as split into **-k/u* + **aṇ* (cf. Ta. *a-v-aṇ* 'there', *naṭu-v-aṇ* 'in the centre', ? Ta. *aṇ* 'upper part').[39] Ka. locative suffix *-alli* is very probably to be connected with Ka. *alli* (*DED*1) 'in that place, there, to that place'.

At the end, it looks as if we are left only with the accusative suffixes which may ultimately be reduced to the shapes (1) **-Vn* and (2) **-ay,* with the dative **(-k)k(V),* and the genitive **-at/u, *-Vn, *-ă̄.* It seems, though, that even some of these most 'grammaticalized' case-suffixes might be etymologized back to a free lexical form. Thus e.g. Andronov sees a connection between the old Ka. accus. and instrum. suffixes *-aṃ* and *-iṃ* and the deictic words **aṃ* 'that' and **iṃ* 'this'[40] (which is, though, not very convincing). The pan-Dravidian dative *-k/u* may perhaps be connected with the verb base **koṭ/u/ *kuṭ/u* 'to give (to 3rd person)' (*DED* 1708); both is, of course, extremely speculative. As J. Bloch says, "on pourrait pousser plus loin ce catalogue et multiplier les hypothèses; c'est affaire de lexique et d'étymologie. Ce qui importe, est de marquer la relative indépendance des éléments flexionnels et la généralité du principe de groupement des mots en composition."

1.1.3.3.3 Is there any evidence to posit a marked nominative case *vis-à-vis* the oblique? I believe there is, though, again, the conclusion is only very hypothetic. Nevertheless it seems that it is possible to suggest that the **-m/*-n* suffix which occurs in some languages in the nominative of some substantives of the non-personal class, and which has been considered part of the stem, should rather be taken as a nominative suffix. Cf. such items as *DED* 3856 Ta. *mar-a-m,* obl. *mar-a-ttu* 'tree, wood', Ma. *maram,* Ko. *marm,* To. *mēṇ,* Ka. Koḍ. Tu. *mara,* Te. *m(r)ānu, m(r)ā̆ku,* Kol. Nk. *māk,* Pa. *meri,* Ga. (Oll.) *mar, marin,* (S) *māren,* Go. *mara, maṛa, maṛā, māra, māṛa, mārnu, marnu,* Koṇḍa *maran* (pl. *marak*), Pe. *mar* (pl. *marku*), Manḍ. *mar* (pl. *marke*), Kui *mrahnu*, *mrānu*, Kuvi *mṛānū*, *mrānu*, *mārnu*, *marnu*, *mara*, Kur. *mann*, Malt. *manu*. The obvious reconstruction yields **maram*/**maran*.

First, in compounds and as attributes, the words in **-a-m*/**-a-n* lose the final nasal and only the stem in *-a-* occurs in such constructions, e.g. Ta. *mara-k-kompu* 'the branch of a tree'. Second, there are OTa. datives where the dative suffix *-kku* is affixed directly to the stem in *-a* after the *-m*/*-n* is lost, cf. *vēḻam* 'elephant': *vēḻa-kku* (*Tolk.* 1533), *nilam* 'land': *nila-kku* (*Tiruk.* 572). Third, the oblique stem of these nouns is formed so that the final nasal disappears, and the 'empty morph' is affixed: *mara-ttu*. Fourth, derivatives are formed from the stems in *-a-*, cf. Ta. *aram* 'virtue' : *ara-vi* 'id.'. Further, in a number of languages, plurals are formed from the stem without the final nasal: Koṇḍa *mara-k*, Kui *mrahka*, Kuvi *mārka* etc. On the other hand, some case-suffixes in OTa. were appended to the (hypothetical) nominative in *-m* (as with other substantives), and only later to the expanded oblique stem, cf. *Puṟ.* 210.3. *neñcamoṭu* 'with the heart' (later *neñca-tt-oṭu*). According to a count performed (for different reasons) by S.V. Shanmugam (cf. *Dravidian Linguistics* [1969], 28-30), there are in Old Ta. texts approx. 170 instances without *-tt-* before sociative suffix (and only 32 instances with *-tt-*) which shows that at that stage of the development of liter. Ta., this way of forming the sociative must have still been very productive. Cf. also such OMa. instances as *tiṟamōṭu* 'with vigour' and *ñālamōṭu* 'with the world'.

Accord. to *Tolk.* 217, in sandhi, a nasal comes in after the names of trees ending in *-a*. This nasal, according to s. 143, will be the homorganic nasal corresponding to the following plosive. We could easily posit a hypothesis that the original ending of these words was a nasal **-m*/**-n*, which 'reappears' in sandhi, though before pause it had disappeared. This *-am*/*-m*/*-ṉ* 'reappearing' in sandhi may be a reflection of a more ancient form of all these words (like *mā* 'mango', *puḷi* 'tamarind', *paṉai* 'palmyra' etc., cf. *Tolk. sūtras* 229, 231, 243, 244 etc.) – of a nominative ending in *-m*/*-n*. It is also a fact that some of these (and other) words get the 'augment' *-a-ttu*, *as if* they had a nominative ending in *-am*, e.g. (*Tolk.s.* 228) *nilā* 'moon(shine)' :: obq. *nilāattu*. Thus it seems that for all these words, we may presume pre-literary forms like **maam*/**maan* 'mango', **puḷiyam* 'tamarind', **nilaam* 'moon(shine)'. If we look at the comparative evidence, this conclusion of positing asterisked forms with a final nasal gets in fact strong support: cf. for **nilāam* Pa. *neliñ*, Ga. (Oll.) *neliṇ*, (S) *neling*, Go. *nalēnj* etc., Kui *ḍānju* etc. For a pre-literary Ta **maam* 'mango' cf. Koḍ. *maŋge*, Kol. *māmḍī*, *māmṛi*, *mānḍi*, Nk. *māmṛi* etc. Without going here into unnecessary details, it is I think clear that we have to posit in these forms an original final **-m*/**-n*, preserved in OTa. sandhi.

All the facts mentioned in 1.1.3.3.3, taken together, seem to make a case for an ancient nominative marker of the substantives of the non-personal class reconstructable as **-m*/**-n*. This seems to be also the conclusion of Glazov

(*IHGT* 134-135) who says that the Ta. nominative morpheme in two allomorphs, *-m* and *-n*, belongs to the "inflectional morphemes" of old Ta.

The foregoing discussion would support Jules Bloch's statement that there are, in Dravidian, fundamentally only "two cases": the *subject case* (nominative), and the *oblique*. Our analysis leads us to a conclusion identical with that stated by Glazov:[41] *the case system is rather 'underdeveloped'.*

1.1.3.4 The following charts give a comparative survey of the case-suffixes for accusative, dative, genitive, instrumental/ablative, locative/ablative and sociative (comitative) in Dr. languages.

1.1.3.5 In spite of the scepticism expressed above, a very tentative attempt at the the reconstruction of PDr case markers will be made in what follows.

1.1.3.5.1 *Accusative.* – The Old. Ta. accusative suffix is *-ai.* Curiously enough, *Tolk. Col.* 104-05 mentions an alloform, viz. *-a*, occurring in poetry; so far, it has not been discovered in any Old. Ta. text. The commentators quote, as *the* instance, various version of the utterance *kaḷiṟu mañcum(ak) kāvalōṉa* (or *kāvalōṉak kaḷiṟañcummē*) 'the elephant will fear (that) watchman'. According to T. P. Meenakshisundaran, *A History of Tamil Language*, 104, *-a* developed from an earlier **-am*, a conclusion which I find difficult to accept. It seems to me to be rather a case of the monophthongization of the final *-ai>-a*, current in many modern Tamil dialects, and occurring in the 'local' usage of some poets(?).

The Tamil-Malayalam *-ai< *-ay*. By the close of the Early Old. Ma. period, *ai* developed into *-e.*[42] Iruḷa, too, has *-e/∞ -ne* as the accus. marker. The Koḍ. accus. *-a* is most probably also a reflex of **-ay* (cf. the Ta. dialectical developments of *-ai>-e/-a* referred to above). Whether the Kui-Kuvi **-i* can be traced to **-ay* is highly problematic, but not quite ruled out, if we accept an old word-final alternation **-ay :-*i* (as possibly revealed in the ending of the verb of the 2. p. sg. in Old Ta., cf. *-i/-ai/-ay, Tolk.Col.* 223) as being relevant in this case. It is also not certain whether the Brahui accus-dat. *-e* is a reflex of **-ay*. It could be considered as a development of **-ay* in some nonaccented, noninitial syllables. If so, this would establish **-ay* as one of the PDr accus. markers. So far, though, **-ay* as accus. marker seems to be restricted to Ta. -Ma., Irula and Kodagu.[43]

1.1.3.5.2 Another, and much more widespread accusative marker which can be reconstructed for PDr is *-(V)*n*, the reflexes of which are found in Toda (*-n* ~ *-ṇ*), Kota (*-n*), Ka. (*-ăn, -ă, -am, -am, -annu, -annu, -na*), Tu. (*-nɨ*), Te. (*-nun/ -n* ~ *-nin, -nu* ~ *-ni*), Koya (*-nni* etc.), Kol. (*-n* ~ *-un*), Nk. (*-n* ~ *un/-on*), Pa. (*-n* ~ *-in*), Ga. (*-n*~ *-in*, *-ŋ* ~*-iŋ*)(?) Koṇḍa (*-ŋ*), (?) Pengo (*-iŋ* ∝ *-aŋ*), Go. (*-un*), Kur. (*-in* ~ *-an* ~ *-n*) and Malto (*-in* ~ *-en* ~ *-n*); in other words, in *all* Dr. languages of all the three main sub-families with the exception of Ta., Ma., Irula, (?) Koḍ., and

TABLE I

	Accus.	Dat.	Gen and Poss.	Instr./Abl.	Loc./Abl	Soc.
Old Ta.	*-ai*	*-ku~-kku*	*-atu/-ātu; -iṉ; -a; -uṭai;* = Obl.	*-āṉ/-āl;* Abl. *-iṉ; -niṉṟu*	*-iṉ/-il;* = Obl.; *-uḷ, -kaṇ* postpos.	*-oṭu/-ōṭu; -uṭaṉ*
LT	*-ai*	*-ku~-kku*	*-atu; -iṉ; -a; uṭai(ya);* = Obl.	*-āl; -koṇṭu*	*-il;* Abl. *-il- niṉṟu; -il-iruntu*	*-oṭu/-ōṭu; -uṭaṉ*
CT	*-e/-a*	*-ku~-ki*	= Obl.; *-o:ṭe; -kiṭṭe*	*-a:le; -koṇṭu*	*-le: ; kiṭṭe;* post-positions; Abl. *-le:rntu*	*-o:ṭa/o:ṭe; -ku:ṭa*
Ir.	*-e/-ne*	*-(k)ke~-(k)kye*	poss. *-(t)tu, -(t)te, -ṭe*	*-a : le*	*-li~-ili;* Abl.*-ilirundu, -irundu*	*-o:ḍe; -tokka*
Ma.	(*-ai*), *-e*	*-ku~-kku -iṉu~-ṉu -iṉṉu~-ṉṉu*	*-iṉ; -uṭai(ya); -uḍe~ -ḍe; -re;* = Obl.	*-āl; -koṇṭu*	*-il, -kal, uḷ ;* = Obl. postpos.; Abl.*-il-niṉṟu, -ilniṉṉu, -innu, -īnna, -nnu*	*-oṭu/-ōṭu*
Ko.	*-n*	*-k~-g*	*-d*	non-hum. *-ār*/hum·+pron. *-āl; -n*	*-l~-ḷ* Abl. *-tr~-ltr*	*-ōṛ*
To.	*-n, -ṇ*	*-k~-g*	*-d∞-n*	*-āl∞-ār∞-iṭ*	*-s̱~-ts̱~-ẕ∞-kiẓ~-giẓ* Abl. *-s̱n/-niḏ*	*-wīṛ; -poḍy*
Old Ka.	*-ǟn, -ǟ, -am, -aṃ*	*-ke~-kke, -ge~-gge*	*-atu; -ā → a*	*-im, -iṃ/-in/-iṃda, -inda(ṃ), -inde, -indu*	*-uḷ/-oḷ -alli, -i, -e*	
LKa.	*-annu, -nu*	*-ke~-kke, -ge~-gge*	*-a*	*-inda; -koṇḍu*	*-alli*	*-oḍane*

TABLE I (Continued)

	Accus.	Dat.	Gen. and Poss.	Instr./Abl.	Loc./Abl.	Soc.
CKa.	*-Ana/ẓ-anna-A~ ~ø*	*-kke~-Age*	*-a, -ā; -d; -in*	*-inda, -linda, -āginda; -koṇḍu*	*-li; -āge; -e*	
Bad.	*-a*	*-ga*	*-a; -uḍaya*	*-enda*	*-ō/-ōga* ∞ -gen.+*-sāre*	*-o:ḍa*
Koḍ.	*-a~-na*	*-kï~-gï*	*-ḍaẓ-ra*	*-koṇḍi;* gen.+ *-kauñja;* Abl. *-iñja;* gen.+ *kayñja*	*-lï∞-alli/-olïli*	gen.+*-pakka,* +*-jotëli,* +*-kūḍa*
Tu.	*-nɨ*	*-kï~-gï*	*-ta~-da∞-na/-a*	*-ṭa~-ḍa;* Abl.*-ttɨ/-ḍḍɨ* (*-ḍudu,* Br.*-ttu, -ntu*)	*-ṭɨ~-ḍɨ∞-oḷu,*Brahm.	*-ṇṭu*
Old Te.	*-nu(n)~-ni(n)/-n*	*-ku(n)~-ki(n)*	*-a; -i; -adu*	*-nan/-n; -cētan;* Abl. *-uṇḍi*	*-nan, -an, -n; -andu; -ḷōn(a)/-lōn(a)*	*-tōḻa(n); -tōḻi; -tōḍa; -tōḍi; -tō(n)*
Te.	*-nu~-ni*	*-ku~-ki*	*-i; -a; -a(du)*	*-ṭa. -ta, -cäeta*	*-lō,* Abl. *-nuṇḍi/ -niñci*	*-tōḍu, -tō*
Koya	*-nni, -minni, -ninni, -i, -ini,*	*-ku~-iki~-ki; -k*	*-i, -ini; -a*	*-e; -i*	*-e; -i,*Abl. *-kāsi; -kunci; -nunci*(<Te.)	*-tōn*
Kol.	*-n~-un*	*-ŋ~-uŋ*	*-e -ne*	*-aḍ~-naḍ* Abl. *-tanaṭ*	*-nadaŋ* sg.∞*-adaŋ* pl.	postp. *-nokon*
NK.	*-n~-un/-on*	*-n, -un*	*-ne/-e; -n*	*-la;* Abl. *-la; -tal; -aṛ* (pron.)	*-tun; -in/-un/-en/-n -(t)el(ti), -ka(n)*	
Pa.	*-n~-in*	*-g~-ug* (N) *-ŋ~-uŋ* (S)	*-n~-in∞ti~-to* (S *-ta*); *-na*	*-oḍ~-noḍ*	*-t-i;* Abl. *-tug*(N)/*-tuŋ* (S); (*t*)*ar*(*e*), *-*(*n*)*ar*(*e*)	

TABLE I (Continued)

	Accus.	Dat.	Gen. and Poss.	Instr./Abl.	Loc./Abl.	Soc.
Ga.	*-n∼-in/ŋ∼-iŋ*	*-ŋ/-uŋ*	*-n, -in/-ŋ, iŋ; -ne; -ṭe* *-ṭ*	*-nāl*	*-t-un∼-t-in, -n, -iŋ* Abl. *-ṭuŋ, -pelṭuŋ*	*-nāl*
Koṇḍa	*-ŋ*	*-ŋ*	*-ti, -di, -Ri, -ni, -ṇi,*	*-an, -aṇḍ, -ŋ*	*-t(u), -d(u), -R(u),* *-to, -ṭo, -ṟo, -i*	*-v-ale*
Pe.	sg.*-iŋ*/pl.*-aŋ*	sg. *-iŋ*/pl. *-aŋ*	*-i*	*-aŋ*	*-o*	
Go.	obl. *-ø∼-ŭn*	= Acc.; *-k*	*-ā∞-vā∞-nā*	*-ē* =	Instr.; Abl. *-āl∞-nāl*	*-thōṟo*
Kui	*-i*	*-gi∼-ki*	= Obl., *-ti, -di,*	Abl. *-ṭi, -ṭeka; -ṛai* *-ṛahi; -ṭai, -ḍai*	*-ta; -a; -ni; -nḍo*	*-ge∼-ke*
Kuvi	*-ti∞-ṇi∞-ʔi*	*-aki/-taki/-ki*	*-ti∞-i∞-ø*	*-tole;* Abl. *-ṭi∞-ki∞* *-haʔa -ṭi*	*-ta∞-ṇa; -o; -tara*	
Kur.	*-in∼-an∼-n*	*-gĕ/-kĕ*	*-gahi, -ghē, -gē,-hē,* *-(g)hai* etc.; *-hi; -ta;* *-ā(?)*	*-trī, -trū* Abl. *-tǐ,* *-(i)ntǐ*	*-nŭ, -nõ:*	
Malt.	*-e∼-in∼-n* *∞-en*	*-ik∼-k∞-e*	*-ki*	*-et∼-it∼-t* Abl. *-ne∞-inte*	*-no∼-eno∼-ino*	
Br.	*-e*	= Acc.; *-ki* 'for'	sg. *-nā*/pl. *-tā*	*-aṭ,* Abl. *-ān*	*-aṭī* 'in' *-āi* 'on'	*-to*

possibly Kui-Kuvi and Br. Though several (and all highly speculative) solutions are possible, the one most plausible seems to be that the 'original' direct object marker in Dravidian is to be reconstructed as *-(V)*n*, that even the Kuvi-Kuvi and Br. vocalic markers are reflexes of this *-*Vn* with the loss of the final nasal consonant, and that *-*ay* is a relatively late innovation in one sub-group of SDr, preserved only in the Proto-Tamil-Koḍagu sub-family.

1.1.3.5.3 *Dative.* - The reconstruction of the dative suffix presents no grave problems. In almost all of the languages the velar plosive occurs, followed by a vowel which, in most cases, is identical with the automatic post-plosive vocalic release *-/*u*. Hence we may possibly reconstruct the dative marker as PDr *-(*k*)*ku*. The -*ĕ̄* occurring in Ka. and Kur. may easily be explained as the clitic *-*ē* which became part of the suffix. Kol., South Pa., Ga., Koṇḍa(?) and Pengo (?) -*ŋ* may have developed out of a cluster *-*n* -*k*/*u* with the loss of the plosive and the preservation of the assimilated nasal. The dative -*ki* found in spoken Ta., Te., Koya (cf. Ir. -(*k*)*kye*) may be easily explained as a case of vocalic assimilation, of 'vowel harmony'. In Br. -*ki* occurs as a purposive ('for'), and this suffix is probably related etymologically with the Dr. dative.

1.1.3.5.4 The reconstruction of the *genitive* markers presents more difficulties. Obviously, various so-called genitive suffixes have different functions; the 'meanings' of the so-called genitive may be, roughly speaking, characterised as (1) adnominal relationship, (2) possessive.

1.1.3.5.4.1 A suffix *-*in* is reconstructable as a marker of adnominal relationship in Ta., Ma., some dialects of Kannaḍa,[44] ? To., ? Kol., ? Naiki, Pa. and Ga., and possibly for Te., Koṇḍa, Pengo, Kui and Kuvi. As certain reflexes of *-*in* we may regard the Ta. -Ma. -*in*, the Pa. -*n* ~ -*in*, and the Ga. -*n*/ -*in* , possibly Te. *i*.

1.1.3.5.4.2 According to *Tolk.*, the genitive suffix is -*atu* which alternates with -*ātu* in Old Ta texts. The same -*atu* is found in ancient Ka. mentioned by Kēśirāja and occurring in the Old Ka. text *Vaḍḍārādhane*, and in the Gulbarga Brahmin dialect.[45] It also occurs in Te. with pronouns. Kota -*d* is obviously a development of *-*atu*, and Kui-Kuvi -*di*, -*ti* seem to be related. Hence we may reconstruct *-*atu* as one of the genitive suffixes, occurring probably first in the pronominal paradigm.

1.1.3.5.4.3 -*a* is attested from a number of languages including OTa., OKa. (though -*ā* is more frequent there), OTe., Bad., Tu., Te., Pa., Kol. Some languages, like OKa., Go. and Br., have -*ā*. Taking into consideration the grammatical meaning and the distribution of this suffix in Old Ta., it seems that a possessive suffix *-*ă̄* may be reconstructed for PDr.

1.1.3.5.4.4 A late SDr (or even later than SDr) innovation is the use of **uṭay* (cf. *DED* 510 Ta. *utai* 'wealth', *utaimai* 'state of possessing, possession etc.'. . . through to Te.) as a marker of a possessive 'case'. *-uṭai* occurs in OTa. and early inscriptional Ma., later developing into *-uṭai-y-a*, coll. Ta. *-o:ṭa*/ *-o:ṭe*. Koḍ. *-raꝏ-ḍa* was brought into connection with **uṭay* by L. V. Ramaswami. Being a very late innovation shared only by Ta. -Ma. and Koḍ., it marks a close relationship among these languages.

1.1.3.5.5 Any attempt at further reconstructions forces us to tread upon a rather slippery ground. Thus an *instrumental* suffix *-ān*/*-āl* occurs no doubt in Ta. and Ma. (though not enumerated in the *Tolk.* as one of the case-suffixes; there is numerous evidence for its ancient occurrence in Old Ta. texts), and the Ga. *-n-āl* may prob. be connected; possibly also the Br. ablative *-ān.* If this is so, we might reconstruct a PDr *-*ān*/**āl.*[46] Te. and Koṇḍa have reflexes of an instrumental *-*an*. Kol. -(*n*)*aḍ* , abl. *-tanaṭ*, Pa. -(*n*)*oḍ* and Br. *-aṭ* seem all to be related. One possible connection of these instrumental suffixes would be with the Ta. etc. *-ŏṭu.*

-**in* occurs as another instrum.-ablative marker in SDr (mentioned in *Tolk. Col.* 77-78 as the 'fifth' case used to express, among other notions, 'separation, detachment, colour, shape, measure, smallness, largeness, superiority, inferiority' – in other words, used in comparing items), in Ta. and Ka.

*-*koṇṭu* (which is the adverbial participle of **koḷ* 'to take, receive') is a typical SDr innovation, cf. Ta. *-koṇṭu*, Ka. *-koṇḍu*, Koḍ. *-koṇḍï.*

The etymological connection of other instrumental suffixes (such as those occurring in Toda, Kurukẖ and Malto) remains so far unknown.

1.1.3.5.6 *-*in*/**il* may probably be reconstructed as the underlying shape of a number of related forms which are markers of a locative function: Ta. *-iṉ*/*-il,* Ir. -(*i*)*li*, Ma. *-il*, Ko. *-l, -ḷ*, To. *-s̱*, Koḍ.*-lï.*

A number of postpositions occur as markers of locative relations, the most widespread among them being undoubtedly reconstructable as *-*uḷ*(*DED* 600 Ta. *uḷ* . . . . Br. *urā*[?], cf. *DED* 853): Ta. *-uḷ* (quoted in *Tolk.Col.* 82), Ka. *-uḷ*/*-oḷ,* Te. *-lō,* Tu. *-oḷu*. Because of Te., and of Kui-Kuvi and Malto *-o,* which may perhaps be related, *-*uḷ* as a locative marker may very probably be reconstructed for PDr. In Ta., both literary and inscriptional, the postposition *-uḷ* has been very productive since the earliest times.

*-*kaṇ* occurs in OTa. and Pa. (*-kan*/*-ka*): *Tolk.Col.* 81 quotes *-kaṇ* as the marker of the 'seventh' (locative) case. For its etymology, cf. 1.1.3.3.2.

Tu. *-ḍa*∾ *-ṭa* may probably be connected with the Ta. loc. postp. *-iṭai* < *-*iṭay* (which alternates with the item *iṭam*/*iṭaṉ* 'place', *DED* 368), but a connection with *-*ŏṭu* is not ruled out.

1.1.3.5.7 The most widespread sociative (comitative) marker can be reconstructed as *-ō̆ṭu which is probably etymologically connected with -uṭaṉ(*DED* 798, cf. 1.1.3.3.2 of this book). The loc. *-ḍu∼-ṭu, -ḍɨ∼-ṭɨ* of Tuḷu may possibly be connected with *-ō̆ṭu; however, a connection with *DED* 368 (**iṭam*) is not ruled out. If Te. * *-tōḍa* <*tōḷa* and Go. *-thōṛō* as well as Kol. *-(n)aḍ*, Pa. *-(n)oḍ* and Br. *-aṭ* can all be connected, then we could possibly reconstructed a PDr *-(*t*)-*ō̆tu* as a comitative marker. Cf. also Koya *-(t)oṇṭe* (with a 'pre-nasalization'?) and *-tōn*, as well as Br. sociative *-to*.

1.1.3.5.8 The following extremely hypothetical underlying system of reconstructed Dravidian case-markers emerges:

Nom.: ∅ and, possibly, *-*m*/*-*n* with non-personal substantives.
Acc.: *-(*V*)*n*.
Dat.: *-(*k*)*ku*.
Gen.: adnominal *-*in*; pronominal *-*atu*; possessive *-*ā̆*.
Instr.: *-*ān*/*-*āl*.
Abl.: *-*in*(?).
Locative: -*-*uḷ*; *-*in*/*-*il*(?); *-*kaṉ*.
Soc. (*Comit.*): *-*ō̆ṭu* or *-(*t*)-*ō̆ṭu*<*-*tō̆ṛV* (? ?).

1.2 NUMERALS

1.2.1 Morphologically, Dr. numerals behave like substantives. They are inflected for case by means of suffixes identical with those occurring in the inflexion of substantives. However, they may be considered to form a sub-class of nouns since they do not have the category of number (with the exception of pronominalized, i.e. personal numerals). Numerals do not agree, in Dr., with the Head in a Quantifier-Head construction in number, e.g. Coll. Ta. *na:lu*[1] *ma:ṭu*[2] *varutu* 'four[1] bull[s][2] are coming[3]': Coll. Ta. *anta*[1] *na:lu*[2] *a:ṇka*[3] 'those[1] four[2] males[3]'. The category of gender occurs only with the first five numerals, cf. e.g. the situation in Parji and Kuruḵẖ:

Parji

Masc.	Fem.	Neut.
okur(i)	*okal(i)*	*okut, okti*
irul	*iral*	*irḍu(k)*
mūvir	*muyal*	*mū̃ḍu(k)*
nelvir	*nelal*	*nālu(k)*
cēvir	*ceyal*	*cē̃du(k)*

Kurukh

Masc.- fem.	Neut.
ort	*oṇḍ/oṇṭā*
irb	*eṇḍ*
nubb (<**m-)	*mūnd*
naib	*nākh*

Apart from Parji and Kurukh, special feminine forms occur in Kol., cf. *iddar* 'two men' : *īral* 'two women' : *indiŋ* 'two things'; in Nk., cf. *iddar* 'two men' : *iraḷ* 'two women' : *indiŋg* 'two things'; in Ga. (Oll.), cf. *irul* 'two men' : *iraḷ* 'two women' : *inḍi* 'two things'. With the numeral 'three' this state of affairs – i.e. special feminine forms – prevails, except in Pa., in Kol. (*muggur : muyal : mūndiŋ*) and Nk. (*muggur : muyaḷ : mūndiŋ*), with the numeral 'four' in Pa., Kol. and Nk. again (cf. Kol. *nalgur* four men' : *nallav* 'four women' : *nāliŋ* 'four things').

Starting from Ga. (S) and Koṇḍa, there is, again, only the distinction masc.- non-masc., e.g. Ga.(S) *nalgur* 'four men' : *nālig* 'four women or things', Koṇḍa *mūyer* 'three men' : *munḍri* 'three women or things'.[47]

Thus, the special feminine forms, limited to Kol., Naikṛi, Ga. (Oll.) and Pa., present a remarkable problem since those languages which manifest a masc.-fem. distinction with substantives (South Dravidian) have no such forms with numerals, while e.g. Pa., which has only a two-gender (masc./non-masc.) contrast with substantives, manifests a rather developed three-gender system in all numerals from 1-5. "Here what is properly a feminine singular form is used also in the case of the plural numbers, and exactly how the usage can have come about is not quite clear".[48]

1.2.2 In a number of languages, such forms, manifesting the gender-category, occur as fillers of the Quantifier slots (as quantitative attributes): cf. Ka. *obba* < *orba* < **oruba* (cf. Ta. *oruvaṉ*) 'one man or person', *ibbaru* 'two persons' : *obba manuṣyanige ibbaru makkaḷ iddaru* (*LSI* 375) 'one man-to two sons were'; Pa. *okur* 'one man', *muyal* 'three women' : *okur manja* 'one man', *muyal cālacil* 'three sisters'.

Ta.-Ma., however, show an entirely different usage: attributively, either the numeral of the neuter (*aḥriṇai*) gender is used, or, in the literary language, a special adjective form of the numeral occurs as attribute. Cf. CT *reṇṭu peṇka* 'two women' just like *reṇṭu ma:ṇavuka* 'two students' and LT *iv-v-iru nūlkaḷ* (with the adjective form of the numeral) 'these two books'.

1.2.3 Reconstruction of Proto-Dravidian yields the following *adjective forms of numerals:* **oru* 'one' adj. before consonant~ **ōr* 'one' adj. before vowel; **iru* 'two' adj. before cons.~ **īr* 'two' adj. before vowel; **muC*/**mū* 'three' adj. before cons.~ **mū* 'three' adj. before vowel; **nāl* 'four' adj.; **cayN* 'five' adj. before cons. ~**cay* 'five' adj. before vowel; *caṟu* 'six' adj. before cons. **cāṟ* 'six' adj. before vowel; **eṛu* 'seven' adj. before cons.~ **ēṛ* 'seven' adj. before vowel; **eṭṭ(u)*~ **eṇ* 'eight' adj.;**toḷ*~ **toṇ* 'nine' adj.; **pat(tu)*~ **pan* 'ten' adj.; **nūṟ(ṟu)* 'hundred' adj. Accord. to *Tolk.* 456, 466 *muv* 'three' occurs before vowels.

1.2.4 The adjectival forms of numerals were widely used in the oldest strata of the literary languages, and some of the non-literary languages have preserved such old constructions; cf. such Old and Middle Ta. constructions as *īraṭi* 'the two feet[of the Lord]'; *munnīr, muṉṉīr* 'three-fold water', *mūvēntar* 'the three kings', *aim-peruṅ-kāppiyam* 'the five great *kāvyas*' with Parji *ir ḍāba muy ḍāba* 'two stories, three stories', *irkocil* 'the two sides'.[49] We may probably agree with Burrow and Bhattacharya[50] that "the full forms . . . were not originally used attributively in Dravidian. For this there existed shorter radical forms . . . ".

1.2.5 Numerals higher than 'ten' are in fact constructions of exactly the type described in 1.2.4, cf. Ta. *irupatu* 'twenty' (i.e. 'two ten[s]'), *mup-patu* 'thirty', *nālpatu, nāṟpatu* 'forty', *aim-patu* 'fifty', *aṟu-patu* 'sixty', *eḻu-patu* 'seventy', *eṇ-patu* 'eighty'. *toṇ-ṇūṟu* 'ninety' is formed subtractively from *nūṟu* 'hundred'. The old morpheme for 'nine' exists in a number of languages and may be reconstructed as **toḷ*~ **toṇ*, cf. Ta. *toḷḷāyiram* '900', *toṇṇūṟu* '90', *toṇṭu* 'nine', Ma. *toḷḷāyiram* '900', *toṇṇūṟu* '90', Ko. *tombat* '90', Ka. *tombattu, tombhattu* '90', Koḍ. *tombadï* '*id.*' Tu. *soṇpa* '*id.*', Te. *tommidi* 'nine', *tombadi* '90', *tommanūṟu* '900', cf. *DED* 2910. A careful consideration of the forms shows that the morph **toḷ*~ **toṇ* must have had a 'full' semantic value of 'nine' since, in some languages, '90' seems to mean '9.10' or '10 determined by 9' (as in Ka. Koḍ. Tu. Te.), while in Ta. Ma. '90' seems to be formed, semantically speaking, as 'deficient hundred' or 'hundred minus *toḷ*', cf. Ta. Ma. *toṇṇūṟu* '90' with e.g. Te. *tombadi* '90'. Thus we get the chart 3.

CHART 3

'90' = '100 - toḷ' *'deficient 100'*	*'90' = '9. 10'*
Ta. *toṇṇūṟu*	Ko. *tombat*, Koḍ. *tombadï*,
Ma. *toṇṇūṟu*	Ka. *tombattu, tombhattu*,
	Tu. *soṇpa*, Te. *tombadi, tombhai*,
	Go. (Pat.) *tombai*
'900' = '1000 - toḷ' *'deficient 1000'*	'900' = '9.100'
Ta. Ma. *toḷḷāyiram*	Te. *tommanūṟu, tommannūru*

Cf. also Ta. *toṇṭu* '9' <**toḷ*+ *-*tu*, i.e. 'proniminalized (adjective) *toḷ*'.

"The other 'nine' " is formed definitely subtractively from 'ten', cf. *DED* 862 Ta. *oṉpatu*, Ma. *ompatu*, Ko. *orbād, onbād*.

1.2.6 "The South Dravidian languages including Telugu allow PDr. numeral morphemes to be reconstructed for a decimal system with basic simplex morphemes for 'one' to 'eight', 'ten' and 'hundred'. 'Nine' is formed subtractively from 'ten'. The basic morpheme for 'thousand' is borrowed from Indo-Aryan and similarly for all morphemes of higher orders than that."[51] The reconstructed substantive neuter forms are clearly morphological complexes containing the neuter suffix **-tu* (1-3, 5, 8, 9, 10) and the derivational suffix **-ku* (4): **onṟu, *iraṇṭu, *mūnṟu, *nālku* (found in two instances in Old Ta., *Perumpāṇāṟṟuppaṭai* 489 and *Akam* 104.6; otherwise, the assimilated form *nānku* occurs), **cayntu, *cāṟu, *ēḻu, *eṭṭu, *toṇṭu, *pattu.*

In the CDr and NDr languages, only the Dr. numerals for 'one' and 'two' exist in *all* of them. Malto, Kuvi and Winfield's Kui as well as Pengo replaced 'three' and all higher numerals by IA loans; 'four' and everything higher was replaced in Brahui (by Iranian forms); 'five' and everything higher in Kuru<u>kh</u>; 'six' and everything higher in Kolami of Emeneau; 'seven' and everything higher in Parji; 'eight' and everything higher in other Kui dialects (Letchmajee, Friend-Pereira) and in Koṇḍa; 'hundred' in Kol. of Adilabad.[52]

1.2.7 A decimal system seems to be established for Dr. However, a few etymological speculations, if accepted, might reveal a more ancient numerical system – an *octogenal* system which had been probably in vogue before the Dravidians accepted the decimal system. If *DED* 670 * *eṭṭu* ∾ **eṇ* 'eight' and *DED* 678 **eṇ* 'number, calculation' can be connected, then 'eight' could have been regarded as the 'number' *par excellence.* Further, if **pat* ∾ **pan* (cf. Te. *pan-* '10' in '19', Ka. *pann-* '10' in '11, 12' etc., *DED* 3236) could be connected with **pal* -V- ∾ **pan* -C- 'many' (*DED* 3289), then 'ten' could have been regarded as 'much, many'. And 'nine', as pointed out, is formed in many languages subtractively from 'ten' either by **toḷ* ~ **toṇ* or by **on* (cf. *DED* 2910 with [?] *DED* 2907 Ta. *toḷ* 'to perforate, bore; become weak; hollow, hole, defect'; and *DED* 862 Ta. *oṉpatu* '9').

From the semantic point of view – as a result of these etymological speculations – the Dr. numerical system would then be as follows: 'one, two, three, four, five, six, seven, number; deficient many (*or* many minus one); many'.

1.3 PRONOUNS

1.3.0 Pronouns are a special subclass of nouns since they are marked for *person* as their typical category, and since, in the 1. p.pl., they have an additional semantic dimension, namely the *inclusive-exclusive* contrast.

1.3.1 Personal pronouns are marked for the category of *person* (1st, 2nd and 3rd), *number* (sg. and pl.) and, in the 3rd persons, for *gender* (two or three genders, according to the structure of the gender-sub-system in the respective language).

1.3.2 The sg. : pl. contrast is expressed by the phonemic contrast between **-n* (sg.) and **-m* (pl.), cf. Ka. *tān* 'he, she, it, in the refl. or reciprocal sense': Ka. *tām* 'they, themselves'. Cf. 1.12.5.

1.3.3.1 The distinction between the features 'inclusive' and 'exclusive' may be formulated as meaning the following: 'inclusive' includes the addressee in the meaning 'we', 'exclusive' excludes the addressee. This category is present in all Dr. languages with the exception of Brahui, modern Kannaḍa, and some dialects of modern Tamil. Iruḷa has lost the category in the pronoun but preserved it (or is it an innovation?) in the verb-system. Old texts in Ka. preserve its traces.[53]

1.3.3.2 The forms are:

Inclusive	Exclusive
OTa. *nām*	*yām, yāṅkaḷ*
Ta. *nām*	*nāṅkaḷ* (obl. *eṅkaḷ-*)
CT *na:ma*	*na:nka*
Ma. *nām*	*ñāṅṅaḷ, ñaṅṅaḷ, ñāḷu; eṅṅaḷ*
Ko. *ām,* obl. *am-*	*ām,* obl. *em-*
To. *ōm*	*em*
OKa. *nām, nāvu,* obl. *nam,*	*ām,* obl. *em-*
Ka. *nāvu*	*āvu, āngaḷ; nāvu*
Koḍ. *naŋga*	*eŋga*
Tu. *namo*	*yeṅkuḷu, yăṅkuḷu, eṅkḷu*
Te. *manamu* < **mā-nām*	*ēmu; nēmu, mēmu*
Kol. *nēnḍ*	*ām*
Nk. *nēm, nēnḍ*	*ām*
Pa. *amor* 'you who are ours'[54]	*ām*
Go. (*namoṭ*), *apul, aplō* (? lw)	*ammăṭ, mammăṭ, măṭ,* etc.
Koṇḍa *māpriyop* 'we two'	*mān*
māṭ(u) incl. (Krishnamurti)	*māp(u)* excl. (Krishnamurti)
Kui *āju.*	*āmu, māmu*
Kuvi *māro, mārrō*	*māmbŭ*
Pe. *āheŋ,* obl. *mā-, maŋg-*	*āpeŋ,* obl. *mā-, maŋg-*
Kur. *nām*	*ēm*
Malt. *nām*	*ēm*

The Br. form *nan* belongs etymologically to *DED* 3019 Ta. *nām* but Br. does not distinguish between the two pronouns, excl. and incl. The Ka. form, too, belongs to *DED* 3019; there is, however, no distinction between 'incl.' : 'excl.' in mod. Kannaḍa. The form is *nāvu*, obl. *nam-* in the standard language, *nā̃vũ* in the colloquial style.

As for the phonemic shapes of the pronouns, except Ko. To. and Te., the *inclusive* pronouns have *n-* initially. Excepting Kol. Nk., the following vowel is *ā* in the nominative and *a* in the oblique. Kota *am-*<**nam-* and Toda *om*<**am*< **nam-* lost their initial nasal. We can reconstruct, therefore, **nām*/**nam-* as the 1. p.pl. inclusive pronoun for Dravidian. The 1. p.pl. exclusive pronoun can obviously be reconstructed as **yām*/**yam-* for. PDr.

1.3.3.3 Tracing the feature back into history we may see that in OTa. texts the distinction 'inclusive' : 'exclusive' is observed in a vaguely general way, but the *Tolkāppiyam* though it notes the coexistence of the two *forms* does not indicate any difference in their use or meaning (*s*. 647). In some modern Ta. dialects, the distinction is observed, but not too rigorously. In medieval Tamil, the incl. *nām* is used, too, as majestatis and auctoris (e.g. in royal grants and administrative papers), and also in soliloquy.

From what was said at the end of 1.3.3.2 it is obvious that the dimension 'inclusive' : 'exclusive' has to be reconstructed as a PDr feature. After the separation of CDr from the rest of the languages, all the CDr languages except Kol. Nk. and Te. have lost the first p. incl. pl. pronoun. The Te. form is historically **mā -*nām > manamu*, while the Kol. and Nk. *nēm, nēnḍ* do not seem to be directly descended from PDr **nām.*[55]

1.3.4 The pronouns of the 3. p. are, etymologivally, 'pronominalized' forms of the deictic (demonstrative) and interrogative *adjectives *a 'that* (remote)', **u*'that (intermediate)', **i* 'this (proximate)' and **yā-*/**ē* 'which (interrogative)'.

The three demonstrative vowel-roots are attested from Ta.-Ma., Ko., Ka., Tu., Pa., Kui-Kuvi, Kur. Malt. and Br. Cf. the following illustrations;

**a-*	**u-*	**i-*
OTa. *a* 'that (remote)'	*u* 'that (interm.)'	*i* 'this (prox.)'
Ma. *a, ā* 'that, yonder'	*u* 'that', *umpar* 'gods'	*i, ī* 'this'
Ko. *avn* 'that man'	*ūn* 'he'	*ivn* 'this man'
Ka. *ā* adj.,*ava* 'that man'	*ū* adj.,*uva* 'this man'	*ī* adj., *iva* 'this man'
Tu. *avu* 'those things'	*undu* 'this thing'	*imbe* 'this man'
Pa. *ōd* 'that man', *at* 'in that direction'	*ūd* 'this male', *ut* 'in that direction'	*id* 'this woman/thing', *it* 'in this direction'
Kui *aanju* 'that man'	*oanju* 'that male'	*ianju* 'this male'
Kuvi *āasi* 'that man'	*ūasi* 'that male'	*īwasi* 'this man'
Kur. *ās* 'that man'	*hūs* 'this male'	*īs* 'this man'

*a-	*u-	*i-
Malt. *athi* 'look there! '	*uthi* 'look there! '	*ithi* 'here! '
Br. *dā, dād* 'this'	*ō, ōd* 'this, that' (interm.)'	*ī-* (*DEDS* 351 a)

Apart from this three-way distinction, Kui-Kuvi has another degree of 'that nearer'; in other words, the Kui-Kuvi subfamily has a *four-way* distinction in the order *i, e, a, o*: Kui *ianju* 'this man (here)', *eanju* 'that man (nearer)', *aanju* 'that man (over there)', *oanju* 'that man (farthest)', cf. *DED* 651. According to *DEDS* 651, the Go. (S), Pe. and Manḍ. forms are etymologically connected, cf. e.g. Pe. *e* 'that', Manḍ. *evan* 'that man'. Go. (SR.) *ūr* 'they' is to be connected with **u-* (*DED* 475). In Brahui, the situation is follows:

*a-	*u-	*i-	*e-
dā, dād 'this'	*ō, ōd* 'this, that (interm.)'	*ī-* 'a base declined for case, to which the enclitic suffix pronouns are added'	*ē* 'that most remote', *ē, ēd* 'that'

The four-way distinctions are limited to Kui-Kuvi and Brahui, but we find traces of this system survive in Pe., Manḍ. and some dialects of Go. The matter is not yet entirely clarified, and it is impossible to say whether the four-way distinction is an innovation, or a preservation of a more 'original', pre-Dr. state. In many languages, the three-way distinction has been abolished through the loss of the intermediate degree (e.g. in Ta. and Ka.)[56]

The 3. p. pronouns are *demonstratives* formed from the demonstrative (deictic) roots by pronominal suffixes. Some forms, e.g. Nk. *avnd* 'that man' or Koṇḍa and OTe. *vānṟ(u)* 'that man' show that we have to reconstruct, for the 3. p.sg. masc., two forms, **avan* and **avanṯ.*[57]

1.3.5 The reflexive pronouns *DED* 2612 Ta. *tāṉ*, pl. *DED* 2582 Ta. *tām* show the same sg. : pl. distinction expressed by the morphs **-n : *-m* as the 1st and the 2nd persons. This fact, and the fact that the reflexive occurs, in some languages and/or historical stages of some languages and/or in some dialects of some languages, in the *function* of a 3. p.sg. and pl. *personal* pronouns, leads us to the conclusion that **tān*, pl. **tām* were originally the 3. p.sg. and pl. *personal* pronouns of Dravidian, with the meaning **tān* 'he, she, it' : **tām* 'they (m., f., n.)'. In some dialects of literary languages, e.g. in some Eastern Ta. local patois, the reflexive still occurs in the function of personal pronoun.[58] The forms **tān, *tām,* functioning as personal pronouns of the 3. p.sg. and pl. had been used, however, in this meaning only in the very early period *before* the gender categories began to be manifested by means of the agreement in gender between the pronoun and the verb.[59] Later these third person pronouns _*tān_ and _*tām_ which do not distinguish gender were replaced by derived pronouns (demonstratives) manifesting the gender-category, and _*tān_, _*tām_ were used more and more as 'pure' reflexives and, still later, as emphatic (indeclinable) particles.[60]

1.3.6 The personal pronouns of the first and second persons were recently discussed by Bh. Krishnamurti and M. Kandappa Chetty.[61] According to Krishnamurti the reconstructions are _*yān_ and _*yām_ for the 1. p.sg. and pl. with the oblique bases _*yan-_ and _*yam-_; and _*nīn_ and _*nīm_ for the 2. p.sg. and pl., with the oblique stems _*nin-_ and _*nim-_. The 1. p.pl. _*ñām_ 'we (incl.)' is explained by Krishnamurti as a phonemic representation of a morphological complex, morphophonemically // _*n- yām_ // 'you and we (excl.)'= 'we (incl.)', i.e. '_*nīn_ + _*yām_'. We tend to agree, however, with M. Kandappa Chetty, according to whom the reconstructed shape of the 1. p.pl. is _*nām_ 'we (incl.)', obl. _*nam-_. The Kol. and Naiki forms with _ē_ seem to be later innovations. There is in fact no conclusive evidence for any form beginning with _*ñ-_ in PDr.

1.3.7 The system of PDr personal pronouns, in terms of a Pike-an matrix, has originally two dimensions with a third dimension added to the first person plural. It may be represented by chart 4 which is structurally very satisfactory in its regular systemicity.

Chart 4

	sg.	pl.
1	_*yān_ : _*yan-_ 'I'	excl. _*yām_ : _*yam_ 'we' / incl. _*nām_ : _*nam-_ 'we'
2	_*nīn_ : _*nin-_ 'you'	_*nīm_ : _*nim-_ 'you'
3	_*tān_ : _*tan-_ 'he, she, it'	_*tām_ : _*tam-_ 'they'

1.3.8.1 Tables III-V give a comparative survey of the 1st and 2nd person pronouns, and of the 3rd personal-reflexive pronouns in Dr. languages.

1.3.8.2 _Tolk. Col._ 162, cf. also _Eḻut._ 193, mentions the two plurals _yām, nām,_ but only one singular, _yāṉ_. In the Ta. literary texts, _nāṉ_ appears only rather late, in the Middle Tamil period. Middle Tamil grammars, _Vīracōḻiyam_ and _Naṉṉūl_, mention _nāṉ_ as the 1. p.sg. pron. besides _yāṉ_. According to G.S. Gai, _ān_ 'I' occurs in Ka. inscriptions from the 7th Cent. onwards; both _ān_ and _nān_ occur in the inscriptions and literary texts from the 10th Cent. According to

TABLE III

1. *person*

Language	singular	plural	
		inclusive	exclusive
OTa.	*yāṉ eṉ-* I	*nām nam-* V	*yām, yāṅ-kaḷ em-* III
Ta.	*nāṉ* II *eṉ-* I	*nām nam-* V	*nāṅkaḷ* IV *eṅ-kaḷ-* III
CT	*na:n* II *e:n-* I	*na:ma nam-* V	*na:nka* IV *enkaḷ-* III
Ma.	*ñān, nān* II *en* I	*nām nam-* V	*ñāṅṅaḷ* IV *eṅṅaḷ-,* III *ñaṅṅaḷ-* IV
Ko.	*ān en-,e-* I	*ām am-* III	*ām em-* III
To.	*ōn en-* I	*om om-* III	*em em-* III
OKa.	*ān en-* I	*ām* III, *nāvu* V *nam-* V	*ām em-* III
Ka.	*nānu nan-* II	*nām, nāvu nam-* V	*nāvu nam-* V
CKa.	*nā̃nu, nā̃ nan-* II	*nā̃vũ nam-* V	*nā̃vũ nam-* V
Koḍ.	*nānï, nā* II *en-* I, *nan-, nā-* II	*naŋga naŋga-* IV	*eŋga eŋga-* III
Tu.	*yānu, yānụ, yēnu, yēnụ en-* I	*nama nam-* V	*yeṅkuḷu, yeṅkuḷe* *yaṅkuḷụ, eṅkḷu yaṅkuḷe-* III
Te.	*ēnu* I *nēnu, nānu nan-, nā-* II	*manamu man-* V	*ēmu* III *mā-* IV *mēmu, nēmu* V

TABLE III (Continued)

1. *person*

language	singular	plural	
		inclusive	exclusive
Kol.	*ān an-* I	*nēṇḍ nēṇḍ-* V	*ām am-* III
Nk.	*ān an-* I	*nēṇḍ, nēm nēṇḍ-* V	*ām am-* III
Nk.(Ch)	*ān an-* I	*ām(e) am-* III	*ām(e) am-* III
Pa.	*ān an-* I	*ām, amor am-* III	*ām am-* III
Ga.(Oll)	*ān an-* I	*ām am-* III	*ām am-* III
Ga(S).	*ān an-* I	*ām am-* III	*ām am-* III
Go.	*na(n)nā̆* *an(n)a* I *na-* II	*aplō aplōt-*	*ammā̆ṭ, ammoṭ* *ammok* III *ma-* IV *namoṭ, nammā̆ṭ, māṭ* etc. IV
Koṇḍa	*nān na-* II	*mān, māp- mā-* IV	*mān mā-* IV
Pe.	*ān/āne* I *na-, naŋg-* II		*ap(e)* III *ma-, maŋg-* IV
Manḍ.	*ān* I		
Kui	*nānu; ānu* I *nā, nan-* II	*āju mā-* IV	*māmu mā-* IV
Kuvi	*nānū̆ nā-* II	*māro, mārrō mā-* IV	*māmbū̆ mā- IV*

TABLE III (Continued)

1. *person*

Language	singular	plural	
		inclusive	exclusive
Kur.	*ēn eṅg-* I	*nām nam-* V	*ēm em-* III
Malt.	*ēn eṅg-* I	*nām nam-* V	*ēm em-* III
Br.	*ī* (?)*kan-* I	*nan nan-* V	*nan nan-* V

TABLE IV
2. person

Language	sg.	pl.
OTa.	*nī nin̲-* I	*nīm, nīr* IIA *num* IIB
Ta.	*nī un̲-* I	*nīr, nīṅkaḷ* IIA *um-, uṅkaḷ-* IIB
CT	*ni: on-* I	*ni:nka* IIA *unkaḷ-* IIB
Ma.	*nī nin-* I	*niṅṅaḷ niṅṅaḷ-* IIA
Ko.	*nī nin-* I	*nīm nim-* IIA
To.	*nī nïn-* I	*nīm nīm-* IIA
OKa.	*nīn nin-* I	*nīm nim-* IIA
Ka.	*nīnu nin-*I	*nīvu, nīṅgaḷ nim-* IIA
CKa.	*nī̆nu, nī̃ nin-* I	*nī̆vũ nim-* IIA
Koḍ.	*nīnī, nī nin-, nī-* I	*niŋga niŋga-* IIA
Tu.	*ī nin-*I	*nikuḷu, nikuḷu̥, nikuḷe-,* IIA
		inkuḷu, īru inkuḷe, īre-,
Te.	*nīvu, īvu nin-, nī-* I	*īru* IIA, *mīru* III *mim-, mī-* III
Kol.	*nīv in-* I	*nīr im-* IIA
Nk.	*nīv in-* I	*nīr im-* IIA
Nk.(Ch)	*nīv, īv in-* I	
Pa.	*īn in-* I	*īm im-* IIA
Ga.(Oll.)	*īn in-* I	*īm im-* IIA
Ga.(S.)	*īn in-* I	*īm im-* IIA
Go.	*ī̆mmā, nimā, nī-* IIC	*immaṭ, nimeṭ* IIC *mī-* III
	nime, nimaṭ etc.	*mīmaṭ, mimeṭ, mī* III
Koṇḍa	*nīn nī-* I	*mīr(u) min-, mī-* III
Pe.	*ēn, ēneŋniŋg-, nī-* I	*ēp, ēpeŋ miŋg-, mī-* III
Manḍ.	*īn* I	*īm* II
Kui	*īnu, nīnu nī-* I	*nīm* IIA, *mīru nim-* IIA
		mīmu III *mī-* III
Kuvi	*nīnū̆ nī-* I	*mīmbū̆, mīru mī-* III
Kur.	*nīn niŋg-* I	*nīm nim-* IIA
Malt.	*nīn nin̲g-* I	*nīm nim-* IIA
Br.	*nī nē-, n-* I	*num num-* IIB

NOTE: The Roman indexes occurring with the 1. and 2. pers. pronouns refer to the 'phonological groups' as given by Krishnamurti in his paper "Dravidian Personal Pronouns" (*Studies in Indian Linguistics*, [1968], 189-205). Observe, also, the innovation shared by Toda and Kota in the oblique forms of the 1. p.pl. exclusive and inclusive (Kota *em-* and *am-*; Toda *em-* and *om-*, the latter < **am-*): M.B. Emeneau, "The South Dravidian Languages", *JAOS* 87:4 (1967), 367.

TABLE V

3. *pers. refl.* (←*personal*)

Language	sg.	pl.
OTa.	*tāṉ taṉ-*	*tām tam*
Ta.	*tāṉ taṉ-*	*tām tam-*
Ma.	*tān tan-*	*tām tam-*
Ko.	*tān tan-/ta-*	*tām tam-*
To.	*tōn tan-*	*tām tam-*
OKa.	*tān tan-*	*tām tam-*
Ka.	*tān(u) tan-*	*tām, tāvu, tam-, tav-*
Koḍ.	*tānï tan-*	*taŋga taŋga-*
Tu.	*tānụ tan-*	
Te.	*tānu tan-*	*tāmu, tamaru, tam- tāru*
Kol.	**tān tan-*	**tām tam-*
Nk.		*tām*
Pa.	*tān tan-*	*tām tam-*
Ga.(Oll.)	*tān tan-*	*tām tam-*
Go.	*tanā, tān tan-*	*tammā, tammaṭ*
Pe.	*tān tā-, taŋg-*	
Kui	*tanū tāṛan-* etc.	*tāru*(m.), *tāi*(n.) *tāṛan-* etc.
Kuvi	*tanū, tānu tan-*	*tambū, tāmbu tam-*
Kur.	*tān taŋg*	*tām tam-*
Malt.	*tān, tāni taṉg-*	*tām, tāmi tam-*
Br.	*tēn*	

Kandappa Chetty (who quotes *Nannaya Padaprayoga Kosamu* [Hyderabad, 1960]), in Nannaya's *Mahābhāratam* only 4 clear cases of *nēnu* 'I' occur while there is a 'large number' of occurrences of *ēnu* 'I'. One explanation of the late occurrence of the forms with initial *n-* is that the Ta. form *yāṉ* (and analogical Ka. and Te. forms) was the form current in the literary dialect, or, at any rate, the 'standard' form, while *nāṉ* (and analogical Ka. and Te. forms) was a form current in some spoken dialect(s) which became accepted as a literary form much later. Another, and probably more plausible explanation, is the explanation by *Systemzwang* and analogy: *yāṉ* remained isolated in the paradigm

**yāṉ : *yām/*nām*
**nīn : *nīm;*

an 'analogical' initial *n-* 'forced itself' upon the 1. p.sg. too. Probably, there was an interaction of both factors.

The isogloss of the loss of initial *n-*, typical for CDr, included a portion of SDr; hence we have such forms as Tamil *uṉ-, um-;* these forms, however, must have also been used early only in the substandard dialects, since they are not found in early classical Tamil texts (cf. the Iruḷa situation). The actual developments were probably rather complex, and included such features as labialization and analogical levelling, too. Some of the developments may probably be symbolized by the following ordered rules:

(1) labialization of the vowel because of *-m: nīm→num;*
(2) loss of initial *n-: num→um;*
(3) transferred by analogy to the sing.: *niṉ→uṉ.*

Iruḷa which is a SDr language closely akin to Old Ta., and which has preserved a number of archaic features, has the following pronominal system:

	Sg.	Pl.
1. p.	*nā, nān : nan-*	*nāmu : nam-*
2. p.	*nī : nin-*	*nīmu : nim-*

The third persons are demonstratives. The additional dimension of 'inclusive-exclusive' is lacking in Iruḷa pronouns, but is preserved (?) in the verb and overtly expressed by different suffixes (*-ēmu* excl.,*-o* incl.).

Taking into consideration the OTa. situation and such archaic Tamiloid language like Iruḷa, the OKa. and OTe. situation, and the state of affairs in other SDr languages, we may probably reconstruct the following pron. system for PSDr:

Sg.	Pl.
1. **yān : *en-*	1.a. **yām : *yam-; *ām* (cf. Ko. To. OKa.);
**ān* (cf. Ko. To. OKa.)	b. **nām : *nam-; *ñām* (cf. Ma.)
**ñān* (cf. Ma.)	
2. **nīn → *nī : *nin-*	2. **nīm- : *nim-*
3. **tān : *tan-*	3. **tām : *tam-*

The reconstructed forms of PCDr are, according to M. Kandappa Chetty, as follows:

Sg.	Pl.
1. **ān : *an-*	1. **ām : *am-*
2. **īn : *in-*	2. **īm : *im-*
3. **tān : *tan-*	3. **tām : *tam-*

According to the same author, the reconstructed Proto-Kurukh-Malto forms are as follows:

Sg.	Pl.
1. **ēn : *eng-*	1.a. **ēm : *em-*
	b. **nām : *nam-*
2. **nīn : *ning-*	2. **nīm : *nim-*
3. **tān : *tan-*	3. **tām : *tam-*

The PDr system was reconstructed in 1.3.7.

1.3.9 *Pronominalized (personal) nouns*

1.3.9.0 In the ancient literary languages, and in a number of modern and non-literary languages of the family, there exists a category, a type of derivation, "unequally distributed in the Dravidian family but characteristic of it"[62] which may be called *personal* or *pronominalized nouns.*[63] It is more or less obvious that this type of derivation can be reconstructed for Proto-Dravidian itself.

1.3.9.1 The first problem to solve is whether we should regard these personal nouns as an independent 'part of speech' (class of words) or not. This problem has been a matter of dispute for a long time. According to ancient Ta. grammarians, the category was considered to be a specific sub-class of *verbs* (*kuṟip-puviṉai,* lit. 'symbolic verb': *kuṟippu* 'mark, sign', *DED* 1533) on the base of its syntactic functioning as predicate. This point of view was adopted by Pope, Lazarus, Rhenius and Caldwell. J. Bloch suggested that they be considered a specific, independent part of speech, inbetween nouns and verbs ("il fournit une transition entre le nom et le verbe", *SGD* 36). However, he obviously regarded them basically as verbs ("ils équivalent dès lors exactement à des verbes", *SGD* 33).

T. Burrow and A. Master criticised Bloch's point of view; however, their own solution does not seem to be valid either. They explained this category as a kind of adjectives which are used either as determinatives or as predicates.[64] Recently, Andronov (*A Standard Grammar of Modern and Classical Tamil* [Madras, 1969]) considers them as a separate part of speech, characteristic of Classical Tamil (p. 122).

According to our conviction, pronominalized nouns (*cum* pronominalized adjectives) belong to a *major hyper-class* of nouns+adjectives+verbs (the NAV hyper-class), this classification being based on identical patterns of behaviour in syntax and morphology (including identical patterns of derivation). But they do not form a separate part of speech. For this conception, cf. constructions like Ta. *nāṉ*[1] *aṭi*[2]*-y-ēṉ*[3] 'I[1] slave[2] – 1. p.sg.[3]' (i.e. 'I am a slave') : *nāṉ*[1] *nal*[2]*-l-ēṉ*[3] 'I[1] good[2] – 1. p.sg.[3]' (i.e. 'I am good'): *nāṉ*[1] *pō*[2]*-v-ēṉ*[3] 'I[1] go[2]-fut. – 1. p.sg.[3]' (i.e. 'I shall go').[65] A form like Ta. *aṭiyēṉ* 'I am a slave' is a pronominalized substantive noun stem; a form like Ta. *nallēṉ* 'I am good' is a pronominalized adjective stem; and a form like Ta. *pōvēṉ* 'I (shall) go' is a 'pronominalized' (future) verb stem. Thus we see that the 'feature of pronominalization' is equally present, and, expressed by an overt morph indicating the categories of person, number and gender, is attached in an identical manner to the noun, adjective, and verb stems. From this point of view we may accept the solution of Glazov (*IHGTL* 152) who says: "Among nouns and adjectives we single out a special *category of predication,* expressed by morphemes differentiable by person and number *structurally identical* to the *pronominal* endings of verb constructions. Nouns, including verbal and participial nouns, function as predicate" (my emphasis).

Hence it is possible to conclude that it is exactly the same process by which the resulting forms are derived from the underlying forms: the underlying forms, belonging to three different parts of speech - nouns (*aṭi* 'slave'), adjectives (*nal* 'good') and verbs (*pō-v-* '[shall] go')' are transformed into pronominalized (personal) forms by an identical process – affixation of pronominal suffixes; the resulting forms may function in sentences as their subjects, objects or predicates. They manifest, primarily, the category of *person* (and, in the third persons, of *gender*). They may be inflected for *number* and *case*.

1.3.9.2. *Instances from various Dr. languages*

1.3.9.2.1 In Old Tamil, the system is well-developed and perfectly productive and symmetrical. The pronominal suffixes are:

Sg.	Pl.
1.p. *-ē̆ṉ*	*-ē̆m, -ā̆m, -ōm*
2.p. *-ai, āy, -ōy*	*-ī̆r*
3.p.m. *-ā̆ṉ, -ōṉ*	
f. *-ā̆ḷ, -ōḷ*	*-ā̆r, -ōr*
n. *-(t)tu*	*-a*

A complete paradigm formed from the adjective base *nal* 'good' is, e.g., *nallēṉ, nallāy, nallāṉ, nallāḷ, naṉṟu* <**nan-tu, nallēm, nallīr, nallār, nalla.*

Instances from Ta. texts: *uri* 'possession, etc.': *uriyaṉ* 'he who has', *uriyōr* 'they who have', *urittu* 'belong-it' (all from *Puṟam*); *uravu* 'strength': *uravōr* 'they who are strong, heroes', *uravōṉ* 'he who is strong, hero' (*Puṟam*); *iḷai* 'youth': *iḷaiyaṉ* 'young-he', *iḷaiyōḷ* 'young-she', *iḷaiyam* 'young-we', *iḷaiyatu* 'small-it', *iḷaiya* 'small-they', *iḷaiyōy* 'you who are young! ', *iḷaiyar* 'young-they, small-they, servants' (all from *Puṟam*); *aṭi* 'foot': *aṭiyēṉ* 'myself (at your) feet, myself (your) slave'; *aṭiyēm* 'we (your) slaves' (*Tiruvācakam*).

Pronominalized nouns formed on compounds or phrases: *āṟṟal-uṭaiyōr* 'those who have strength, valour; heroes' (*Puṟam* 13.5); *kaḷiṟṟu-micaiyōṉ* 'he who is on top of the male elephant' (*Puṟ.* 13.4). Frequently, the noun or adjective receives a vocative suffix: *tēvar→tēvar-īr* 'oh, you god(s)!'; *peru*> *periyōṉ→periyōṉē* 'oh, you great one! '

In Old and Middle Tamil, personal nouns were regularly susceptible to declension. Instances: *tēvarīruṭaiya* (gen. possess.) *taṉitāṉattil* 'in your presence, o god! ' (*Tiruvācakam*); *tēvarīraip pukaḻntu* 'having praised you, o god! ' (accus., *ibid.*); *pāviyēṉaip* (accus.) *paṇikoṇṭāy* 'you have taken me to be (your) servant, me, the sinful one' (*pāvi-ēṉ-ai, ibid.*); *perumpūṇēṉukku* (dat.) 'to me who has a great ornament' (J. Bloch).

In Modern Tamil, however, just like in Mod. Kannaḍa, only the personal nouns of the 3. p. are still active; the system as such disintegrated, since the opposition in person was annulled. Hence, the personal nouns of the 3. p. lost their pronominal character and became a sub-type of substantives, characterized by the derivational suffixes **-tu* (sg.): **-a* (pl.) : *nal* adj. 'good' : *nallatu* 'good-thing, good-it', *nalla* 'good-things, good-they'; *uḷ* 'existence': *uṇṭu* < **uḷ-tu* 'it exists, it is, it is had (with dat. *alicui est*)'; *al* 'be not so-and-so': *allatu* 'it is not so-and-so (but different)' > 'or'.

1.3.9.2.2 In Ka., we have traces of a system which must have been probably as widespread and regular as that of Old and Middle Tamil. These traces remain in the pronominalized forms of numerals: LKa. *obbanu*/CKa. *ɔbnu* 'one male person': LKa. *obbaḷu*/CKa. *ɔbḷu* 'one female person' : LKa. *obbaru*/ CKa. *ɔbru* 'one respected person', *ibbaru*/*ibru* 'two persons', *mūvaru* 'three persons' etc. Cf. further *ondu pustaka* (CKa. *und pustga*) 'one book' (where *ondu*/*und* is the pronominalized substantive form of the numeral used attributively), *nāvu ibbarū* (*LSI* 379) 'we two' (or rather 'we both'). As mentioned above, the pronominalization of adjectives and of a very limited number of substantives (like *uṭai* 'possession': *uṭaittu* 'that which has' or *pāl* 'side; nature': *pāṟṟu* 'that which is appropriate') has been productive even in modern Ta., but only with regard to to the 3. p.sg. and pl. (cf. modern spoken Ta. *avanka ciriyavanka* ← **av-ar-kaḷ ciṟ-i-y-a-v-ar-kaḷ* 'those persons [are] small'). This derivation is productive also in modern Ka., cf. *avar-alli chikkavanu* (*LSI* 375) 'the younger-one of those persons' (< *cikka* 'little, small, young', *DED* 2075), *hos(a)b-a* 'male stranger': *hos(a)b-(a)ḷ/u* 'female stranger',[66] as well as in a number of other Dr. languages, cf. e.g. Te. *cinnadi* 'girl, lass', *cinnavā̃ḍu* 'boy, young man'< *cinna* 'small, little, young', *DED* 2135, and *ibid*.Pa. *cind, cinḍ* 'son'<*cin* 'little', Ga. Oll. *sinḍ*, S. *cinḍu*, *sinḍu* 'small' < *sin*. In Old Ka., we have, on the one hand, numerals used attributively in both adjective and substantive (i.e. pronominalized) forms (cf. *ōr āḻke* 'one rule' besides *ondu paṇamam* 'one [sum of] money', *ay mattal* 'five measures' besides *aydu varisakke* 'for five years', where the first type corresponds to classical and literary Ta., while the second type corresponds to modern and spoken Ta.), on the other hand 'appellative nouns of number'[67] like *orvvan* 'one person', *pannirbbar* '12 people', *mūvar-ā* 'of 3 persons'. We even have, and that is most important, traces of personal (pronominalized) *nouns: indabaḷḷiyātan* 'the man of Indabaḷḷi' (8th cent.), *madengeḻeyaru* 'the people of Madengeḻe' (9th cent.)[68] J. Bloch quotes *magaḷa maganeṃ* 'je (suis) le fils de la fille', *peṇḍatiyeṃ* 'je (suis) la femme'.

1.3.9.2.3 In CDr languages, too, the pronominalization of nouns and adjectives is a widely, albeit an unequally distributed phenomenon. J. Bloch (*SGD* 29) quotes a number of instances from Trench (of 'enclitic forms of the pronouns affixed to the predicates'), and it seems that in Go. the personal derivation is extremely productice. Cf. *anā*[1] *koitu-nā*[2] *āndan*[3] 'I[1] Gond-I[2] I -am[3]', *ammaṭ*[1] *vartāl*[2] *-ōr*[3] *-ām*[4] 'we[1] guest[2]-pl.[3]-are[4]', *immā cuḍḍō-nī andī* 'you sg. are the one who is young'.

In recently published account of Koya (Gommu Dialect), S.A. Tyler gives the following description of what happens in that language: "All qualitative adjectives, possessive pronouns, the verbal adjective . . . , adverbs of time and place . . . , numerals . . . , and the question word 'what' (bāta) may be converted to nouns by the suffix //TI//. //TI// has allomorphs /ṭi/, /ṭ/, /di/. /ṭi/ occurs after numerals, qualitative adjectives, and adverbs of time and place. /ṭ/ occurs after postpositions. /di/ occurs elsewhere."[69] Tyler calls the process 'nominalizations' and gives, e.g., the following instances: *tiyya> tiyyaṭi* 'sweet thing', *nēṇḍu* 'day' > *nēṇṭi* 'day it', *bāta* 'what'> *bātādi* 'what it', *nā* 'my'>

nādi 'my it', *nāvi* 'my things'.

In Pa., again, the derivation seems to be vigorously productive with adjectives,[70] cf. *ān vilen āy* 'I am white', *ī pūvul vilov āy* 'these flowers are white', (< *vil* 'white', *DED* 4524); *netrocilin ender* 'bring the red ones' (<*netro* 'bright red'< *netir* 'blood', *DED* 3106); *pened veñed* 'the new man has come', *punovin ender* 'bring the new ones' (< *pun* 'new', *DED* 3511); *iled*, pl. *ilenkul* 'young man': *ile*, pl. *ilecil* 'young women' (< *ile* 'young', *DED* 436). The same usage is found with pronominal adjectives, cf. *īta* 'such like this': *īten* 'I am like this', *ōd īted* 'he is like this', *īter* 'such persons'.

Kui pronominalizes nouns and adjectives (as well as pronouns) forming 'appellative nouns' like *tōṛenju* 'male friend' (< *tōṛe* 'friend, friendship', *tōṛu* friendship', *DED* 2939) : *tōṛali* 'female friend', *kūenju* 'Kūi man' (< *kūi* 'the Khond tribe or language ', *DED* 1811) : *kūali* 'Kūi woman', cf. *āmu kūinga-n-amu* 'we are Kūi people'. Cf. further (with adjectives) *neganju* 'good man' : *negari* 'good woman or thing' (and with pronouns) *nāanju* 'my man' : *nāndi* 'my woman, my thing' : *nāaru* 'my men' : *nāi* 'my things' (e.g. *eanju nānda ōtenju* 'he took mine',[71] where we may quite easily recognize the pronominalizing suffixes *-anju* (< **-anṯ/u*) masc. : *-ndi* non-masc. : *-aru* (< **-ar*) pl. masc. : *-i* (< **-i*) pl. non-masc.

1.3.9.2.4 It is an important fact that personal nouns occur systemically in North Dravidian as well. J. Bloch[72] gives a number of Kuru<u>kh</u> examples; *ēn kūṛux-an, ēn kūṛuxni-n* 'je (suis) un, une Kurukh', *ām pāph-am* 'nous (sommes) pécheur', *īd endr xōcol? āl-gahi-d* 'qu'est cet os? Humain' (*gahi-* 'de', *āl* 'homme'). According to Hahn,[73] personal nouns (which he calls 'appellative verbs') may be found formed "by conjugating nouns, adjectives and the possessive case form of nouns" and this formation is obviously quite productive, cf. such instances as *nīn kuru<u>kh</u>ai* 'thou art an Orão' : *nīm kuru<u>kh</u>ar* 'you are Orãos' (nouns), *ās kōhas* 'he is great' : *ār kōhar* 'they are great' (adjective), *ēn rancintan* 'I am the Rancī one' : *ēm rancintam* 'we are the Rancī ones' (possessive case form of noun); cf. also *ēm*[1] *tang*[2] *<u>kh</u>addam*[3] 'we[1] (are) his[2] son(s)-we[3]', *malyan* 'I am not the one', *talyan* 'I am the one'.

In Malto, pronominalized nouns are current, too, cf. *ēn maqen* 'I (am) child-I' : *nīn maqe* 'you-sg. (are) child-you'. As in some other languages (e.g. Kui-Kuvi), pronominalized nouns in Malto are also formed on derived stems, so that the pronominalization is a higher-level derivation. This fact can be demonstrated on numerals. The adj. form of 'one' is *ort*, a form derived from the adj. base *or-*; it is used attributively in e.g. *ort-maqi* 'one girl' (cf. *iwr maqer* 'two sons'). A further derivation – the pronominalization – generates the forms *ort-e* 'one man' : *ort-i* 'one woman', *iwr-er* 'they two'.[74]

1.3.9.3 Thus even from a fragmentary and sketchy account like the foregoing, one is bound to conclude that the type of derivation called personal alias pronominalized nouns is widely distributed in SDr, CDr and NDr, and hence *should obviously be reconstructed for PDr* as one of the very typical grammatical, structural features of the family. The details, however, remain to be worked out ; at present, an exact statement is probably impossible.

NOTES

1 The terms 'surface' and 'phonetic' structures are employed in this utterance in a rather specific sense – the one given to them by Wallace L. Chafe, *Meaning and the Structure of Language* (Chicago and London, 1970). By employing these terms, we want to indicate that we tacitly adopt the fundamental features of Chafe's model of language, which seems to us very attractive. The basic properties of this model may be symbolized by the following scheme, describing the Tamil phrase *ilaiyiluṭkāra* 'to sit to eat'. (See page 58).

The data dealt with in this book are limited to the 'phonetic' structure of Dravidian (in Chafe's sense) which manifests the surface structure of the languages in question. It is our opinion that, at this stage of the development of Dravidian studies, we have to gather, classify and describe the data as they appear in the phonetic output manifesting the surface structure, before we can deal with the immensely complex relations between the semantic and postsemantic structures as manifested by various postsemantic processes, and before we can even begin to reach out to the semantic structure of Dravidian.

2 E. g. the alternation of short and long radical vowels (and/or consonants) in derivation, as in *DED* 2958 Ta. *naṭu* 'to set up' : *nāṭṭu* 'to set up', *DED* 973(a) Ka. *kaṇ* 'eye' : 1209 Ka. *kāṇ* 'to see', *DED* 3191 Tu. *paḍẹyuni* 'to feel, experience, etc.' : Tu. *pāḍu* 'likeness, form, etc.'; or the alternation of long/short root vowels in verbal flexion, as in *DED* 2002 Ta. *cā* 'to die': past stem *cett-* < **catt-*, *DED* 1209 Koḍ. *kāṇ* 'to see': past stem *kaṇḍ-*.

3 For the regular morphophonemic alternation in Dravidian bases cf. Bh. Krishnamurti, "The History of Vowel-Length in Telugu Verbal Bases", *JAOS* 75 (1955), 237-52; *id.*, *Telugu Verbal Bases* (Berkeley, 1961), 121-22; M.B. Emeneau, "Sketch of Dravidian Comparative Phonology" (mimeo, Berkeley, 1963); K. Zvelebil, "On Morphophonemic Rules of Dravidian Bases", *Linguistics* 32 (1967), 87-95; *id.*, *Comparative Dravidian Phonology*, The Hague-Paris, Mouton, (1970), Appendix I, 184-187.

4 It is perfectly possible for a language to change its typological character in the course of its historical development, and some processes of this kind (probably from a more 'synthetic' structure to a more 'analytic' structure) might have taken place in the Dr. family.

5 The prefixes occurring in IA loan-words are of course not to be regarded as prefixes in the borrowing languages.

6 For the hypothesis of monosyllabic roots in Dravidian cf. Bh. Krishnamurti (1955, 1961) and further K. Zvelebil, Yu. Glazov, M. Andronov, *Intoduction to the Historical Grammar of the Tamil Language* (Moscow, 1967), ftn. 5 on pp. 93-94, and pp. 115-116.

7 Owing to frequent metathesis in some languages, some of the alveolar and cacuminal consonants occur initially in these languages, e.g. in Te. (cf. forms like *rōlu, ṟōlu* 'mortar' < **uralu, lō* 'in, inside' < **ula-* < **uḷḷa-*), Kol. (cf. *ḍig-* 'to descend' < **iḻ -g-*), Kui (*leti* 'soft' < **iḷ-a-y, ḍēnju* 'to be raised' < **eḻu-*), Kuvi (*rikhali* 'to unroll' < **vri-* < **viri-*) etc.

8 For an exception, cf. OTa. *uriň* 'to rub against' (*Tol̇k.s.* 80, *Iḷampūraṇam* comm.).

9 M.B. Emeneau has shown that we have most probably to reconstruct this non-morphemic final *-u* for PDr, cf. his "Koḍagu Vowels", *JAOS* 90:1 (1970), 153.

10 Cf. Yu. Ya. Glazov, "Morphemic Analysis of the Language of Tirukkuṟaḷ", in *IHGTL* pp. 113-114.

11 Cf. Glazov "Morphemic Analysis", 14-16. Nouns , adjectives and verbs form a single major NAV class based on similar behaviour in constructions like Ta. *nāṉ aṭiyēṉ* 'I am a slave' (subst.): *nāṉ nallēṉ* 'I am good' (adj.): *nāṉ pōvēṉ* 'I shall go' (verb). This phenomenon – when nouns are concerned – is sometimes called 'conjugation of nouns' (and adjectives); J. Bloch has termed the resulting forms 'pronominalized nouns' (*noms pronomina-*

nalisées), S.G. Rudin has coined for them the term *personal nouns* and *personal adjectives.*

12 A path-breaking study of echo-words in Dr. was performed by M.B. Emeneau who read in 1937, his paper "Echo-words in Toda" at the 9th All-India Oriental Conference at Trivandrum (cf. *Collected Papers* by M.B. Emeneau [Annamalainagar, 1967], 37-45).

13 This would agree well with the more recent classification of Kui-Kuvi as "the earliest identifiable off-shoot of the Dravidian tree" (M.B. Emeneau, *Brahui and Dravidian Comparative Grammar* [1962], 70). However, in a personal communication, Emeneau now seems to have abandoned his early reasons for making this statement about Kui-Kuvi. Nevertheless, he still thinks he is on the right track as far as the archaic nature of Kui-Kuvi is concerned, and this is the important matter for us here.

14 *CGD* (ed. 1913), 220.

15 M.S. Andronov, *DJ* (1965), 48.

16 J. Bloch, *SGD* (Paris, 1946), M.B. Emeneau, *Kolami* (ed. 1961, 148-149). While Bloch considers type [3] as "l'état le plus ancien", Emeneau is inclined to consider type [2] as original.

17 Bh. Krishnamurti, *TVB* (Berkeley, 1961) 256.

18 T. Burrow, S. Bhattacharya, *The Parji Language* (Hertford, 1953), 9. Arguments "ab intra" may indeed lead us to the conclusion that a 'natural' three-gender system may have originally prevailed in Dr. The superimposed, sophisticated division into *uyartiṇai : aḵriṇai*, if and when taken as 'rational' : 'ir-rational', seems to be clearly a later innovation of ancient Ta. grammarians. If, on the other hand, taken as a basic dichotomy between 'humans' and 'non-humans' (i.e. 'personal' vs. 'non-personal') it may indeed reflect a very ancient categorization of entities. The hypothesis of an original two-gender system (masculine : non-masculine) was also proposed by A.S. Kedilaya ("Gender in Dravidian", *Dravidian Linguistics* [Annamalainagar, 1969], 169-176). According to P.S. Subrahmanyam ("The Gender and Number Categories in Dravidian", *Journ. Annamalai Univ.*, 26 [1969], "The Central Dravidian Languages", *JAOS* 89:4 [1969], 739-740), it is the Te. and the Kuruḵẖ-Malto system which must be attributed to Proto-Dravidian. His arguments sound very convincing. Cf. also an interesting paper by K. Kushalappa Gowda, "Gender Distinction in Gowda-Kannada" (*Studies in Indian Linguistics* [1968], 212-20). Further, H. Willman-Grabówska, " La catégorie du genre dans les langues dravidiennes", *Biuletyn polskiego towarzystwa językoznawczego* 11 (1952), 162-70.

19 M.B. Emeneau, *Brahui and Dravidian Comparative Grammar* (Berkeley and Los Angeles, 1962), § 4.14, p. 56.

20 M.S. Andronov, *DJ* (1965), 49. Cf. also his "Lichnye formy glagola v sovremennom tamil'skom jazyke", *Jazyki Indii* (Moskva, 1961), 372-77.

21 According to Andronov, this morph is a contamination of two suffixes, **-k* and **-l(u)/-*-ḷ(u)*, cf. his "Dravidian Languages", *Archiv Orientální* 31 (1963), 185, 190-91.

22 Morphophonemically, the *-ḷ* appears before vowels: *janankaḷe* 'people (accus.)' and before the loc. suff. *-le*:, cf. *marankaḷḷe*: 'in the trees'.

23 H.M. Nayak, *Kannada Literary and Colloquial* (Mysore, 1967), 76.

24 Cf. F.B.J. Kuiper, *Nahali, A Comparative Study* (Amsterdam, 1962).

25 J. Bloch, *SGD* (1946), 8-10.

26 S. Bhattacharya, "Naiki of Chanda", *IIJ* 5 (1961), 88.

27 M.S. Andronov, *DJ* 51. For excellent arguments concerning the reconstructions of this pl. marker, cf. P.S. Subrahmanyam, "The Gender and Number Categories in Dravidian", *Journ. of Annamalai Univ.* (1969), 79-100, and "The Central Dravidian Languages", *JAOS* (1969), 746-47.

28 P.S. Subrahmanyam, "The Central Dravidian Languages", *JAOS* 89 (1969), 739-50.

29 Subrahmanyam, "The Central Dr. Languages", p. 748.

30 For the Old Tamil plural, cf. *Tolk. Col*. 169-and 171. Cf. further K. Zvelebil, "*Iṉṉā-nāṟpatu*: A Study in Late Old Tamil Philology", *AO* (1957), 56-82, esp. 61; L.V. Ramaswami Aiyar, "Notes on Dravidian", *IHQ* 4 (1928), 596.

31 The empty morphs were termed "inflectional increments" by Caldwell (1875), 156-66, "Bindesilben" by Beythan (*Praktische Grammatik der Tamilsprache* [Leipzig, 1943]), "stem formatives" by M.Shanmugam Pillai ("Tamil Literary and Colloquial", *LDSA*, 27-

42), "formative suffixes" by M.B. Emeneau (*Kolami* [1955]), "augments" by M. Andronov (*DJ* [1965], 53) who follows the usage of K.V. Subbayya and L.V. Ramaswami Aiyar, and "flective increments" by Glazov (*IHGT* [1967], 135). They do not express any grammatical or lexical meaning and can be incorporated in morphophonemic rules (H.M.S. Nayak, *Kannada Literary and Colloquial* [1967], 74). In using the term "empty morphs" I follow Ch. F. Hockett ("Problems of Morphemic Analysis", *Lg.* [1947], 321-43), supported by the indigenous Ta. grammatical term *cāriyai* = *cārntu varum iṭaiccol,* derived from *cār DED* 2030 'to depend upon, lean on, rely upon' + *iyai DED* 399 'to join' (see *Tolkāppiyam ss.* 119, 120ff., *Nannul* s. 126). According to *Tolk.* 120, the *cāriyai* are *iṉ, vaṟṟu, attu, am, oṉ, āṉ, akku, ikku* and *aṉ,* but there are other [words, *piṟavum*] used as empty morphs. According to some authors, these morphs "have lost their original significance" since, accord. to *Tolk.* as interpreted *par exemple* by T.P. Meenakshisundaran, "they help us to understand the meaning" (perhaps of the case signs). Caldwell thought they were old case sings ([1956], 259). Cf. T.P. Meenakshisundaran, *HTL* (1965), 76-78, 92-93, 98, 101-102, 124, 153-155. Cf. also M. Shanmugam Pillai, "Ca: riyai vaṟṟu of Tolka:ppiyam", *IL* 25 (1964), 105-107 and T.P. Meenakshisundaran, "The so-called Inflectional Increments in Tamil", *IL* 20 (1959), 125-30.

32 The distribution of the various suffixes is of course not freely alternating. It is primarily conditioned systemically according to the style (whether formal, literary or informal, colloquial) and, of course, morphophonemically. However, these details cannot be worked out in this sketch. For detailes concerning the distribution of inflexional suffixes in Ka., cf. e.g. H.M.S. Nayak, *Kannada Literary and Colloquial* (1967), 77-78, and W. Bright, *An Outline of Colloquial Kannada* (1958), 35-36.

33 "Les cas grammaticaux" or "les désinences grammaticales" in opposition to "les désinences à sens réel" of J. Bloch (*SGD* [1946, 16).

34 Cf. K. Zvelebil, "Dative in Early Old Tamil", *IIJ* (1958), 54-56.

35 In OTa., there exists e.g. a regularly recurring postposition with a sharply definable function and meaning, which could be regarded as a 'case-suffix' of, let us say, the 'relative' case (*-vayiṉ* 'in relation to, relative to, towards, on,upon' : *vayiṉ* 'belly, stomach, womb, centre, inner space, etc.' *DED* 4299), cf. *Puṟam* 210.6-7 *emvayiṉ uḷḷātiruttal* 'not thinking on us'. Or, there is another regularly recurring postposition or clitic *-toṟu/-tōṟu,* which was described as forming a "case" called "distributive", cf. S.V. Subramanian, *Descriptive Grammar of Cilappatikaram* (Madras, 1965), p. 65: *maṉaitoṟu* 'every house', *ūḻitōṟu* 'every aeon'. In fact, we could posit, for Old Ta., not eight but at least ten or even eleven 'cases' (nominative, objective, instrumental, sociative, dative, ablative-comparative, genitive-possessive, locative, relative, distributive, vocative); and, if necessary, we could even distinguish between different types of locatives, and thus probably increase our number of cases to the notorious eighteen.

36 *IHGTL* (1967), 23. Also, J. Bloch, *SGD* 12.

37 *IHGTL* (1967), 23, and ftn. 47. Cf. also J. Bloch, *SGD* 12.

38 *IHGTL* (1967), 137.

39 J. Bloch, *SGD* 17.

40 M. Andronov, *DJ* 56.

41 *IHGTL* (1967), 151.

42 A.C. Sekhar, *Evolution of Malayalam* (1953), 67.

43 In fact it seems that we have to establish a 'Proto-Tamil-Koḍagu' sub-group within the SDr sub-family. There are a few isoglosses marking either shared innovations or shared retentions in Koḍagu, Ta. and Ma. A number of important features connects Koḍ. with SDr minus Kannaḍa. Among the striking phonological features common to Koḍ. and Ta.-Ma. belongs, first of all, the preservation of the cluster 'homorganic nasal plus occlusive' (whereas Ka., Ko. and To. show reduction of the cluster), cf. Ta. Ma. *pāmpu,* Koḍ. *pāmbï* : Ko. *pāb*, To. *pōb*, Ka. *pāvu*; second, Koḍ., unlike Ka. but in agreement with Ta.-Ma., does preserve the qualities of *e* and *o* when followed by *i, u,* cf. Ta. Ma. Koḍ. *eli* 'rat' : Ka. *ili*, Ta. Ma. Koḍ. *oḷi* 'hide' : Ka. *uḷi*. As a morphological preservation, shared by Old and Lit. Ta. and Koḍ., one should point out the small verbal sub-class with the canonical form CV̆y and the past stem suffix **-t-* : Lit. Ta. *cey, ceyt-, ceyv-* 'to do, make' : Koḍ. *key, kejj-* (< **keyj-* < **keyt-*). Among the innovations, common to Koḍ. and Ta.-Ma., one

should point out, apart from a sub-class of verbs with the future morph *-pp-* and the past morph *-nt-*, the genitive-possessive in **uṭai(ya)*, and, possibly, the accusative in **-ay*. (For the Koḍ. features in verb-morphology and their relevance for the genetic position of Koḍ., cf. M.B. Emeneau, "The South Dravidian Languages", *JAOS* 87:4 [1967], 365-413. For the genetic position of Koḍ., cf. also K. Zvelebil, "From Proto-South Dravidian to Malayalam", *AO* 38 [1970], 51-52.)

Let me use this opportunity to suggest here a new stemma for SDr which takes into account the recent discussions concerning the position of Tuḷu and Koḍagu within the Dr. family:

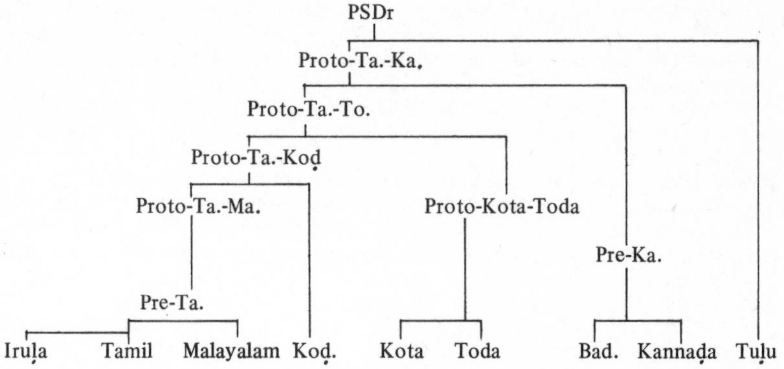

(The best discussion of the position of Tuḷu as to date was offered by P.S. Subrahmanyam in "The Position of Tuḷu in Dravidian", *Ind.Ling.* 29 [1968], 47-66.)

44 Cf. W. Bright, *An Outline of Colloquial Kannada* (1958), p. 32: *gurvin mane* 'the guru's house'.

45 "It is to be pointed out that Ke:sira:ja, the native Kannada grammarian has referred to the suffix -atu without assigning any meaning to it. But it is clear from his example that it is a genitive case suffix occurring after personal pronoun . . . There is one instance of – -adu with first pronoun i.e. ennadu in vaḍḍa:ra:dhane" (S.V. Shanmugam, "Case System in Dravidian", [Annamamalainagar, 1970], xeroxed). For the Gulbarga dialect, cf. R. Mahadevan, *Gulburga Kannada* (Brahmin Dialect), (Poona, 1968).

46 For the alternation **-n-/*-l-*, cf. K. Zvelebil, *Comparative Dravidian Phonology*, 1.28.5, p. 132.

47 Krishnamurti's forms (*Konda or Kūbi*, [1969], 247) are *mu -'er: mūnṟi*.

48 T. Burrow and S. Bhattacharya, *The Parji Language* (1953), 36.

49 T. Burrow and S. Bhattacharya, *The Parji Language* (1953), 37.

50 *The Parji Language* 37.

51 M.B. Emeneau, "Numerals in Comparative Linguistics (with special reference to Dravidian)", *Bulletin of the Institute of History and Philosophy* (= *Academia Sinica* 29) (1954) 1-10. Cf. further R. Radhakrishnan, "Tamil Numerals", *IL* 24 (1963), 87-122, S.V. Shanmugam, "Tamil Numerals", *Proceedings of the 1st Intern. Confer. of Tamil Studies* II (Kuala Lumpur, 1969), 729-34, and G.K. Panikkar, "Dravidian Numeral Constructions", *DL* (1969), 203-17.

52 M.B. Emeneau, "Numerals . . . ", p. 145, supplied by recent data for Pengo and Koṇḍa.

53 G.S. Gai, *Bull. Deccan College Research Institute* I (1940), 411ff. According to Emeneau, "The South Dravidian Languages", (*JAOS* 87:4 [1967], 391), Badaga has two pronouns, excl. *eŋga* and incl. *naŋga.*

54 Burrow and Bhattacharya, *The Parji Language*, 40.

55 For details, cf. M. Kandappa Chetty's excellent paper "Personal and Reflexive Pronouns in Dravidian", *Annamalai University Seminar on Dravidian Linguistics* II (1970), xerox. According to Kandappa Chetty, CDr, after its separation from PDr, lost its initial *n-* in all its pronouns, and hence we have to reconstruct **ām/*am-* for PCDr. After the

metathesis in Te. and Go., the nasal was again shifted to the initial position in the obl. forms which resulted in an innovation favouring initial nasals, i.e. Te. *nēmu, mēmu,* Go. *nammăṭ* etc.

56 For the interrogative base, cf. *DED, DEDS* 4228. For detailed discussion of the Brahui phenomena, cf. M.B. Emeneau, "Brahui Demonstrative Pronouns", *JAS* 3 (1961), 1-5, and entries 1, 351(a), 475, 651 and S 59 of *DEDS*. There is yet another dimension to pers. pronouns in a number of Dr. languages – that of different degrees of 'politeness'. Since, however, this dimension has developed quite obviously independently in each of the languages or small sub-groups of languages, and no over-all Dr. system can be reconstructed, it is of no direct concern to us here. For illustration, cf. the modern spoken 'standard' Telugu, as described e.g. by Krishnamurti, which has four degrees of politeness: 1. *wāḍu* 'he (familiar,impolite)'; 2. *atanu* 'he (polite)'; 3. *āyana* 'he (respectful)'; 4. *wāru* 'he (very respectful)'. In the dimension 'remote-proximate', all these pronouns refer to 'remote'; the corresponding proximate forms are *wīḍu, itanu, īyana, wīru.*

57. Cf. M.B. Emeneau, *Kolami,a Dravidian Language* (1951), 147. For a discussion of the demonstrative and interrogative vowels and the respective derived pronouns, cf. J. Bloch, *SGD* 18-22.

58 Cf. Kamil Zvelebil, "Personal Pronouns in Tamil and Dravidian", *IIJ* 6 (1962), 65-69. The conclusions reached in this paper about the reconstructed phonemic shapes of the 1. and 2. p. pronouns in PDr are now considered by the author to be doubtful, although they may probably offer an alternative to Krishnamurti's reconstruction. However, there is additional evidence for considering **tān,* pl. **tām* as originally personal pronouns: cf. M. Kandappa Chetty ("Personal and Reflexive Pronouns", 23): the kinship terms of Kuru<u>kh</u> and Tamil (cf. Kur. *taṅg-dadas* 'his elder brother', Ta. *tantai*< **tam-tai* 'their father'), and some compound forms of Te. and Ka. (cf. Te. *atanu* 'he [remote, polite]'< **ā – *tānu,* Ka. *āta* 'he [remote]', *ita* 'he [proximate]').

59 Very tentatively speaking, we may imagine a paradigm in some form of early Dravidian running like this:

**yān keyvu* 'I do'	**yām keyvu* 'we do'
**nīn keyvu* 'you sg. do'	**nīm keyvu* 'you pl. do'
**tān keyvu* 'he, she, it does'	**tām keyvu* 'they do'

The amount of speculation involved in reconstructing utterances like this is naturally still enormous. However, a 'game' like this may be useful for those who would like, e.g. , to 'read' the Indus Valley inscriptions as Proto-Dravidian.

60 Cf. T.P. Meenakshisundaran, *A History of Tamil Language* (1965), 155.

61 Bh. Krishnamurti, "Dravidian Personal Pronouns" (*Studies in Indian Linguistics* [Annamalainagar-Poona, 1968], 189-205; and M. Kandappa Chetty, "Personal and Reflexive Pronouns in Dravidian", xeroxed, *Annamalai University Seminar on Dravidian Linguistics* II (1970).

62 "inégalement répandu dans la famille dravidienne, mais caractéristique" (J.Bloch, *SGD* 29).

63 The term *personal nouns* seems to have been coined by S.G. Rudin (personal communication, 1959 in Leningrad), and employed by Andronov (*DJ* 60) and others. The term *pronominalized nouns* was definitely coined by Bloch (*noms pronominalisées).* This category was also termed 'symbolic verb' (Winslow), 'indefinite or indirect verb' (Lazarus), 'appellative verb' (*Tamil Lexicon*), 'conjugated appellative' (Pope), 'Konjugation "nichtverbaler" Ausdrücke' (Beythan), 'verbalised noun' (T.P. Meenakshisundaram) etc. According to *Tolkāppiyam*, there are two kinds of *predicates*: (1) *viṉai* or the verb (al predicate) proper (later grammarians: *terinilai viṉai*): (2) *kuṟippu* (or *kuṟippuviṉai*), i.e. predicates which show the tense by implication from the context (cf. e.g. *Tolk.* 719).

64 Cf. T. Burrow in *BSO(A)S* 12 (1947), 254-255; A. Master in *JRAS* (1949), 106-07.

65 It is obvious that we have to distinguish between sets of the so-called parts of speech (i.e. classes of word-stems), and (hierarchically) higher 'hyper-classes' (as larger sets of units), to account for identical patterns of morpho-syntactic behaviour of such units. Form-classes of stems which show similar patterns of behaviour in derivation/inflection,

or in syntax, or in borh, constitute a 'part of speech'. In these terms, the Dr. part-of-speech system (including the higher hyperclasses) may be formalized as follows:

A. Inflected Stems			
(1) Nouns	a. Substantives	NA hyper-class	NAV hyper-class
	b. Numerals		
	c. Pronouns		
(2) Adjectives			
(3) Verbs		AV hyper-class	
B. Uninflected Stems			
(4) Particles	a. proper b. enclitics c. adverbs d. interjections e. onomatopoetic words f. echo-words		

66 W. Bright, *An Outline of Colloquial Kannada,* 27.
67 G.S. Gai, *Historical Grammar of Old Kannada* (1946), 74.
68 Gai, *Historical Grammar,* 75.
69 *Koya: An Outline Grammar* (1969), 73.
70 Burrow and Bhattacharya, *The Parji Language,* 32.
71 W.W. Winfield, *A Grammar of the Kui Language* (1928), 51.
72 *SGD* 29.
73 *Kuruk̲h̲ Grammar*, 73-75.
74 The derivation with the morph **-(t)t-* plus pronominalizing suffixes **-Vn* (masc.), **-i* (fem.) must be a very deep and ancient feature common to the entire family: cf. Ta. *oruttan̲* 'one male person' : *orutti* 'one female person'; Ma. *oruttan*, *orutti*; Tu. *ori* 'one man': *orti* 'one woman'; Koṇḍa *oren, orenr̲e* 'one man'; Kur. *or·t* 'one man or woman'. For *iwrer*, cf. e.g. Ta. *iruvar,* Ka. *irvar*, Tu. *irveru̥*, Te. *iruvuru*. Can the Malt. *iwr* be explained as metathesis < **iwr* 'two persons' < **iwr-er* (> *iwrer*) < ***iruvar*?

semantic structure
'to sit to eat'

→ postsemantic process: literalization

postsemantic structure
'to sit in the leaf'

→ postsemantic process: linearization

surface structure
'leaf-in to-sit'

→ postsemantic process: symbolization

underlying phonological structure
ilai-il uṭkār-a

→ postsemantic process: phonological processes

phonetic structure
[ilɛyiluṭka:rɐ]

→ phonemicization and written representation

graphemic structure
ilayil uṭkāra

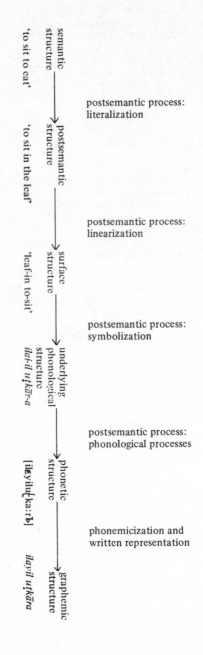

2. ADJECTIVES

Two facts are quite obviously recognizable about adjectives in Dravidian: first, that there exists a separate class of words ('part of speech') in Dr. which may be termed 'adjectives'; second, that 'primary', underived adjectives are, in statistical terms, rather rare in any Dr. language.

2.1 DEFINITION

For Dr. in general, the following definition of adjectives is very probably valid: Adjectives are words which are in attributive construction with a noun they precede; they do not agree with the head noun either in gender or number.[1] Adjectives are *monomorphemic* or *complex*. Monomorphemic adjectives (i.e. stems unanalyzable into constituent morphemes) include *demonstrative* adjectives, *numeral* adjectives, and *descriptive* (or qualitative) adjectives.

2.1.1 As soon as we adopt this position, the whole dispute as to wether there exist 'true' adjectives in Dravidian or not seems futile, and the solution quite obvious: there are adjectives – as defined above – in Dravidian. Not only that: there exist monomorphemic, 'primary', *underived adjectives in all Dravidian languages*; such primary adjectives ('primary' in the sense of linguistic primes) are emphatically *not* derived from nouns and/or verbs, even in diachronic terms.[2] What more, there is nothing to warrant the hypothesis (proposed, e.g., by M. Andronov)[3] that adjectives are not to be reconstructed for PDr; that, in PDr, there was a super-class of nouns which included descriptive words (or, to put it differently, that the function of adjectives was fully performed by nouns in attributive construction with other nouns). On the contrary: there is a limited number of monomorphemic stems which may be reconstructed for PDr as 'primary', i.e. non-derived adjectives. Such are, among others: _*put/u/ *pun_ 'new': cf. Ta. *putu, putiya,* Ma. *putu*, Ko. *pud*, To. *pu, pun*, Ka. *posa*, Tu. *posa,* Pa. *pun,* Ga. (Oll.) *punc,* Go. *punō, punā* etc., Kui-Kuvi *pūni,* Kur. *punā,* Malt. *pune,* Br. *pūskun.* It is the adjective stem, which is 'original', 'primary', and the verbs and/or nouns are secondary, derived: e.g. Ta. *putukku* or *putuppi* 'to renovate', *putumai* 'newness', Koḍ. *pudume* 'wonder' etc. (*DED* 3511).[4] _*ke-/*kē- // *keC-/*kēC-_ 'red': Ta. *ce-, cem-, cev-, ceyya* etc., Ma. *ce-, cem-, cēya,* Ko. *ken, kēt,* To. *kö-,* Ka. *ke-, keṃ,* Koḍ. *kem-,* Te. *ceṃ-,* Pa. *key*, Kur. *k̲h̲ē̆s-*, Malt. *qēs-*, Br. *k̲h̲īs-un. DED* 1607.

**kiṯ-/*kil-* 'small, some, few': Ta. *ciṟu, cil,* Ma. *ceṟu, ciṟ-, cila,* Ko. *kir; kil-,* To. *kïṟ; kïsf,* Ka. *kiṟi, kiṟa, kiṟu, kela,* Koḍ. *kïr-, cer-,* Tu. *kiri, kiru; kela,* Te. *ciṟu, cil-,* Kol. *cil-,* Ga. (Oll.) *sir-,* Go. *kiṛ-. DED* 1308, 1326.

DED 1607 is very interesting: the C is probably equal to **m/*v//*c/*y*. The palatalization is limited only to Ta.-Ma. (and Te.), and is a very late development. Hence, any equation with the name of the god Śiva is ruled out. For the semi-free to free status of an adjective like this cf. the following phrases: Ta. *cen-nāy* 'brown coloured dog, *Canis dukhunensis'* (semi-free), Ma. *cemmīn* 'prawn' (semi-free), Ko. *ken āv* 'red cow', *ke nāy* 'wild dog' (free), Koḍ. *kem-buttī* 'red anthill' (semi-free), Pa. *key cōra* 'dark red pot' (free).

2.1.2 In 1946, Jules Bloch wrote (*SGD* 32) : "il n'y a pas d'adjectifs proprement dits en dravidien; leur rôle est normalement tenu: (1) par la compositi-on . . . (2) par l'emploi de formes rattachées au verbes . . . qui sont à vrai dire d'origine nominale . . ." This mistaken statement of Bloch was rightly objected to by A. Master[5] and T. Burrow.[6] According to R.G. Harshe (the English translator of Bloch's *SGD* [1954]), J. Bloch responded to this critique: "Adjectives are nouns inflected in case and gender in congruence with other nouns. This implies a good lesson in general linguistics. Both have thought as Englishmen, viz., using a language where the epithet is not inflected (good man/men, woman/women, things); they have forgotten about Latin ans Sanskrit . . . But I, as a Frenchman, am aware of the distinction." This whole controversy implies indeed a lesson in linguistics; however, it was J. Bloch who was the victim of his 'inflectional', Indo-European, and more specifically Latin and French-oriented prejudice. For it is *the* property of Dr. adjectives *not* to agree with the head noun they precede in gender or number. In spite of this fact, we have to to consider adjectives as a special class of words whose behaviour differs both morphologically and syntactically from the behaviour of nouns: adjectives are not inflected for case and number like nouns, nor can they be subjects of clauses like nouns. Nonetheless, they form a larger Noun-Adjective set based on similarities in syntactic behaviour, such as Ta. *atu poṉ* 'that (is) gold' : *atu poṉ-ṉakaram* 'that (is) gold(en) town' just like *atu putu nakaram* 'that (is) new town'. But observe that a sentence like **atu putu* which would match *atu poṉ* is impossible.[7]

2.1.3 In this section, I shall give instances of the *use* of *monomorphemic* adjectives in different Dr. languages (including Kuru<u>kh</u>).[8]

2.1.3.1 *Primary Descriptive Adjectives.* – Cf. Tamil utterances like *ciṟu*[1] *talai*[2] *navvip*[3] *peruṅ*[4] *kaṇ*[5] *māp*[5] *piṇai* 'the large[4] eye(d)[5] female[7] – deer[6] [with her] small[1] head(ed)[2] young ones[3]' (*Puṟam* 2.21); *putuc*[1]*-cēri*[2] 'new[1]-town[2]' i.e. Pondichéry; *iṉ*[1] *col*[2] 'sweet[1] word[2], sweet speech', *iṉ*[1]*ṯamiḻ*[2] 'sweet Tamil' (cf. in *DED* 451 [a]); *maṟu nāḷ* 'next day, tomorrow' (*DED* 3903); *vēṟu iṭattil* 'elsewhere' (cf. *vēṟu DED* 4564). All these adjectives are primary, monomorphemic stems, like e.g. Ta. *iṉ* 'sweet', Ka. *in* '*id.*', Ta. *iṉ-i* 'be sweet', *iṉ-pu* 'sweetness', Ma. *in-i-ma* 'pleasure', Ka. *in-i, in-e, im-pu* < **in-pu* etc. 'sweetness', Tu. *im-pu* 'pleasantness', Te. *in-cu* 'to be agreeable', *im-pu* 'sweetness', Kur. *em-bā* 'a taste', Malt. *em-be* 'sweet; sweetness', Br. *hanēn* 'sweet' (*DED* 451 a,b). Surely the structure of these items is quite transparent; they are ultimately derived by means of various suffixes (*-i, -pu, -cu* etc.) from the monomorphemic, monosyllabic root **in-* —→ adj. **in* 'sweet', like in Ta. *iṉ col* 'sweet speech'.

For Ma., cf. *cempon* 'red gold',[9] *peru makkaḷ* 'great people' (*ibid*).

For Kannaḍa, cf. e.g. *kar-g-gal* (8th cent) 'black stone', *beḷ-goḍe* 'white 'umbrella' (10th cent.), *nal-giri* 'good mountain' (7th cent.).[10] For mod. Ka., cf. *cikka mane* 'small house', *hos mane* 'new house', *doḍḍa mane* 'big house'.[11]

For Ko. and To., cf. e.g. Ko. *pūc gīṇ* 'she who has blue eyes' (*pūc* 'blue' + *kaṇ* 'eye[s]' + *y* 'female person'); To. *pūc* 'blue-grey'.[12]

Te. has also a few 'primary' adjectives still in use, e.g. *adi pedda bangaḷā* 'that is a big bungalow' (*DED* 3613), *idi cinna peṭṭe* 'this is a small box'.[13]

More important, primary adjectives are found as active formations in Old Telugu, e.g. *pĕr*, *pen* 'big' (cf. *pen bāṟa* 'great brahmin', 8th cent.), *ciṟu* 'small' (cf. *jiṟudeṟaḷ* 'minor taxes', 927 A.D.).[14]

With regard to CDr, let me quote a few instances from Kolami, Pengo, Parji, Koya and Kui. According to Emeneau, only very few monomorphemic qualitative adjectives are found in Kolami; he quotes *doo* 'big, great' (*DED* 2875 Ta. *toṭṭa*), *telmi* 'white' (prob. < **teḷ-*, a verb, *DED* 2825), *pulle* 'sour' (prob. < **puḷ-*, a verb, *DED* 3546) and *kolāv* 'Kolam'.

As for Pengo, Burrow and Bhattacharya[15] give a list of 23 "native Pengo adjectives" such as, *pazi* 'green, fresh' (*DEDS* 3161), *pṛān* 'old' (*DEDS* 3296), *pūn* (*DEDS* 3511) 'new'.

"Parji preserves a small number of monosyllabic adjectives of the Old Dravidian type",[16] e.g. *pun ole* 'new house', *vil manja* 'white man', *key cōra* 'dark red pot', *pay meram* 'green grass', *koṛ pāp* 'young baby'.

Koya instances may be found in Tyler's recent account of that language,[17] cf. e.g. *erra guḍḍa* 'red cloth', *cinna ōṇḍu* 'small he', *kotta guḍḍa* 'new cloth'. Tyler gives the following monomorphemic qualitative adjectives: *cinna*∼*cinni* 'small, little', *periya* 'large, big', *menci*∼*manci* 'good', *nalla* 'black', *tella* 'white', *erra* 'red', *pulle* 'sour', *tiyya*∼*tīya* 'sweet'. Though one may disagree with Tyler about the 'monomorphemicity' of his instances (at least in terms of comparative and historical approach), yet it is clear that the instances he gives are of 'genuine' adjectives. The same is true about Winfield's account of Kui who gives on p. 34 of his grammar the following items as "other words" used mainly as adjectives": *deri* 'large', *kogi* 'small', *kogeri* 'small', *negi* 'good', *pṛādi* 'old', *puni* 'new'. Of these at least the last three are 'true' adjectives (even if not monomorphemic, i.e. they are derived from underlying monomorphemic adjective stem), cf. Kui *pūni* 'new' with Ta. *putu,* Malt. *pune* (*DED* 3511) < **put/u/*pun*, and Kuvi *pṛādi* 'old' with Ta. *paḻ-a* etc. (*DED* 3296). Of a special interest is Kui *negi* 'good' as compared with Pa. *neŋget, nika,* Ga. (Oll.) *niya,* (S) *niyāṭ,* Go. *nehnā, nihnā,* Koṇḍa *negi,* Kuvi *nehi, nihi* (*DED* 3096).

In Kuruḵẖ, some stems have seemingly preserved what is being considered an extremely ancient state of affairs when the formal and semantic distinction between a noun and an adjective was non-existent, and the context alone determined the meaning. So, e.g., *ūḵẖā* 'darkness': *ūḵẖā māḵẖā* 'dark night' : *ūḵẖī* 'it is getting dark', *ūḵẖyā* 'it has become dark', *ūḵẖō* 'it will get dark'. Apart from the fact that one might argue that all these items are derivations from an 'adjective' stem **ūḵẖ,* and apart from the entirely speculative nature of the 'original' non-existence of adjectives, if words like *ūḵẖā* are 'primarily' nouns used attributely, this is no specific feature of Kuruḵẖ. This is certainly true of all Dr. languages, cf. e.g. the Tamil attributive use and pronominalization of nouns like *poṉ* 'gold' : *poṉ-n-aṭi* 'gold(en) feet' : *poṉṉēṉ* 'I (am) gold(en)'. On the other hand, in Kur., as in any other Dr. language, there exist 'primary' adjectives *from* which nouns (usually abstract) *are derived*: cf. *ās punā eṛpā kamcas* 'he has built a new house', *dau kicrin ondr'ā̌* 'good cloth bring'; other primary Kuruḵẖ adjectives are probably *puḍḍā, puḍḍā* 'short (not tall)' (*DED* 3498), *pacca* 'old' (*DED* 3296) and *khě̃so* 'red'≁blood' (*DED* 1607).[18] It is of course true that according to the existing accounts of the language, Kuruḵẖ seems to have an exceptionally small number of underived adjectives.

Sir Denys de Bray gives quite a list of 'primary' adjectives; he says: "The adjective in its crude form is as a rule either a monosyllable or a dissyllabic compound of a root and an ending."[19] He then quotes 32 monosyllabic adjectives, most of them, if not all, loanwords. What seem to be Br. primary adjectives of Dr. origin (not monomorphemic, though) are *cun-ak* 'small' (*DED* 2135), *ḵẖīs-un* 'red' (*DED* 1607), *pūs-kun* 'new' (*DED* 3511), *mut-kun* 'old' (*DED* 4057) and a few others.

It is evident, however, that, as a category and an independent part of speech, adjectives do exist even in Brahui, cf. an utterance like *chuno chukkas* 'a small bird' (<*chun*+indefinite- *o*).

Hence, we may conclude: it seems that in all Dr. languages, we may set up descriptive, qualitative adjectives as a separate class of words.

2.1.3.1 There is ample evidence from all Dr. languages for the use of *monomorphemic demonstrative adjectives.* For Ta., cf. OTa. *a-p-poruḷ* 'that meaning' (*Tolk.Col.* 16), *a-m-ū-v-iṭattum* 'in all those three positions' (*Tolk.Col.* 28), *i-c-curam* 'this desert' (*Akanāṉūṟu* 8.17), *i-m-maḷaikkē* 'to this raincloud' (*Naṟṟiṇai* 112.9), Mod. Ta. *i-c-cūttirattai* 'this sūtra-accus.', *i-m-mū-vakai* 'these three kinds', *a-t-toṭai* 'that *toṭai*'.[20] For Ma., cf. e.g. *a -vv-āṇṭu* 'that year' (10th cent.), *i-vv-ūr* 'this village' (12th cent), *i-n-nel* 'this paddy' (13th cent.); for Ka., *ī kallu* 'this stone' (9th cent.), *ā nāḍa* 'that country' (8th cent.)[2] Te. has *ī* and *ā,* cf. *ā pustakam* 'that book', *ī peṭṭe* 'this box'; the same is found in Pa., cf. *ā meri* 'that tree', *ī meri* 'this tree', and in Ga. (Oll.), cf. *ī nette* 'this dog', *ā/āy māsil* 'those girls'. Kui has four grades *ī, ē, ā, ō,* cf. *ō kōḍi* 'that cow yonder', *ī vaḍinga* 'these stones here', *ē lāvenju* 'that young man'.[22] For NDr, cf. e.g. Kur. *ā ālasin ērā* 'see that man', *ī mukkan ērā* 'see this woman', and Br. *dā zāiǰe hamē bandag͟hto mon ēte* 'send this woman with that man' (*hamē<ham+-ē*).[23]

2.1.3.2 For monomorphemic numeral adjectives, cf. 1.2.3 and 1.2.4.

2.1.4 In almost all Dr. languages, *polymorphemic, complex adjectives* exists which are derived from nominal, verbal or adjective stems by means of a number of suffixes. Consider, e.g., the situation in Koya[24]: In this language, complex adjectives consist of verbal adjectives and 'derivative' (Tyler's term) adjectives, and they are formed by adding adjectival suffixes to noun or verb stems, e.g. *pacca* 'greenness' : *paccana* 'green', *paccati* 'green' (*DED* 3161); *balamu* 'strength' : *balamana* 'strong', *balamatta* 'strong' (*DED* 4317); for verbal adjectives, cf. *kēnjāni* 'which hears, listens' (*DED* 1677), *dāyova* 'which did not go'.

2.1.4.1 As far as such derived adjectives are concerned, the most widely spread derivational suffix throughout the family is **-a*, which derives secondary from primary, monomorphemic adjective stems as well as from substantives (and, very probably, from verb-stems, too). Consider such cases as OTa. *pal* 'many' in constructions like *paṉ malar* 'many blossoms' (*-l* goes to *-ṉ* before *m-*, *Naṟṟiṇai* 119.6), *paṉ malai* 'many hills' (*Puṟam* 147.1)>*pal-a* 'many' (*DED* 3289, which omits the form *pal*). The same suffix derives secondary adjectives from underlying adjective stems in *-/u*; certain derivational and morphophonemic rules must be applied. Let us consider a derived adjective like Ta. *ciṟiya* 'small'. The pertinent ordered rules seem to be as follows:

(1) *u→i* (*ciṟu→*ciṟi-*, cf. *ciṟi-tu* 'small-it');
(2) add derivational *-a*: **ciṟi-a*;
(3) insert hiatus-filler *-y-*: *ciṟiya*.

The adjective derivative *a* is not limited only to Tamil; it occurs in Malayalam, Kannaḍa, Koḍagu(?), Tuḷu, Telugu and some other languages. Cf. the following instances: Ma. *putiya* 'new' (< *putu*), *paḻaya* 'old, ancient' (< *paḻa*); Ka. *periya* (8th cent.), *piriya* (10th cent.) 'great', *cikka* 'little, small', Koḍ. *ceryë* 'small' (< **cer-* < **kiṟ-*), *nallë* 'good' (< *nal*). In Koḍ., however, more complicated developments seem to be involved: according to Emeneau, the mid back unrounded *-ë* is prob. a development of **-en* and **-an* after the loss of the nasal, cf. Koḍ. *kïrkë* 'small' : Ma. *ceṟukkan* 'boy', so that the Koḍ. *ceryë* < **ceryan, nallë* < **nallan.* Cf. further Tu. *periya* 'large, great', *doḍḍa* 'big' (< **doḍ-*, cf. Ko. *doḍ* 'big, great'< **toṭ-*); Te. *cinna* 'small, little' (< **cin-*), *tella* 'white, pale, clear' (< **tel-* < **teḷ* v.), Pa. *tirra* 'sweet', *pulla* 'sour' etc.[25]

An adjective base which shows neatly the different layers of derivation is

DED 4317 Ta. *val* 'strong, hard'; in a few languages the same monosyllabic sequence of phonemes functions as monomorphemic adjective, cf. Ma. *val*, Ko. *val* 'strong, powerful' (cf. Ko. *val kay* 'right hand'), To. *pas̱* <**val* 'right'. The derivational *-a* occurs, on the first level of derivation, in Ta. *val-a-k-kai* 'right hand', Ka. *bal-a* 'right', Te. *val-a 'id.'*, Pa. *vel-a key* 'right hand', and, on a higher level of derivation, in Ta. Ma. *val-i-y-a* 'strong'. A number of other adjective-derivational suffixes occur with this root, cf. Ma. *val-u* 'strong', Kuvi *bra-i-y-ū* (< **bari-y-ū* < **bal-i-* <**val-i-*), Malt. *bal-ehne* 'large', Br. *bal-un* 'big, large'. Verbs and substantives are formed from the adjective base: Ta. *val-l-am*, *val-l-ai* 'strength', *val-l-u* 'to be able', *val-am*/ *val-an̠* 'strength etc.', *val-i* 'strength, power; be strong', etc., Ko. *val*(*n*) 'man who is clever at cheating', To. *pal-y-* '(child) becomes strong', Ka. *bal-i* 'to increase', Te. *val-am-u* 'largeness, stoutness', *valanu* 'skill', *valacu* 'be capable' etc. It is clear that all these items, occurring in entry *DED* 4317, have to be ultimately derived from the *adjective* stem, reconstructable from PDr, i.e. **val* 'strong' (cf. Skt. *bala-* 'strength').

The investigation of ancient texts shows beyond any doubt that the derivative or rather derived adjectives in *-a* are secondary and relatively recent. In the Old Tamil texts, primary, monomorphemic adjectives are still in productive use while the forms ending in *-a* function as pronominalized adjectives> adjective nouns of 3. p.plural neuter. For the use of primary adjectives as qualifiers in OTa., cf. such phrases as *nal kūrmai* (*Pur̠.* 266.13) 'abject poverty', *peru vir̠al* (*ibid.*266.6) 'great streng', *putu malar* (*ibid.*147.8) 'new blossom', *am-mā-v-arivai* (*ibid.*147.5) 'beautiful dark woman', *tol cuvar* (*ibid.* 211.19) 'old wall', *cen nā* (< *cem nā, ibid.*211.14) 'straight, excellent tongue'.

The morph *-a* which derives pronominalized nouns of 3. p.pl. neuter (cf. *pur̠att-a, Tirukkur̠aḷ* 39.2 'those [which are] outside'), and which, with verb-stems (past and non-past), forms the 3. p.pl. neuter (cf. *iyan̠r̠an̠a* 'those which are created', *alla* 'those which are not so-and-so')[26] is most probably indentical with the adjective derivational suffix *-a*, cf. such early Old Ta. forms as *nalla* 'they (which are) good' (*Pur̠.* 7.9, 37.13, 58.24, 106.1 etc.), *periya* 'they (which are) big' (*Pur̠.* 365.2),[27] *cir̠iya* 'they (which are) small' (*Pur̠.* 235.1)[28]. We may thus most probably accept the hypothesis which derives these secondary adjectives in *-a* from the 3. p.pl. neuter substantives, after they ceased to be used in the substantive function (i.e. after the desintegration of the systemic contrast in the sub-system of pronominalized nouns).[29]

2.1.4.2 Apart from the derivational **-a*, there exists a number of vocalic suffixes which seem to fulfill the function of adjective-derivational morphs. It is too early to point out the relationship, but it seems that a number of languages shares adjective-derivational **-i*;apart from this vowel, *-u, -e* and*-ŏ̄* also occur in adjective-derivational function. Instances:

-i: rather productive e.g. in Parji and Kui-Kuvi, cf. Pa. *guḍḍi* 'black' (no cer-

tain etymology, but prob. < *guḍ-, cf. Go. (M.) guḍ, (Ko.) guḍ-i 'id.), *purki* 'timid' (*DED* 3450), *munḍi* 'short' (*DED* 4047), *lāṭi* 'long' (prob. <*lāṭ-, cf. Go. M. Ma. *lāṭ 'id.', DEDS S*841), *karbi, karbito* 'whole'. Cf. further Kui *negi* 'good' (< *neg-*, e.g. *negi mrānu* 'good tree': *neg-anju* 'good man', *DED* 3096), *pradi* 'old' (*DED* 3296), *pūni* 'new' (*DED* 3511), Kuvi *nihi, nehi* 'good' (*DED* 3096), *prā'i* 'old' (*DED* 3296), Konda *negi* 'good', Pengo *icki* 'small', *krogi* 'fresh', *vari* 'empty', Te. *pir̲iki* 'timed', *manci* 'good'.

-o occurs, e.g., in Pa. *edo* 'good' (cf. *ed-a* Pa.S. '*id.*', and *ed-ka* 'very', *DEDS* 722), *netro* 'red' (? < **netVr* 'blood'), Pengo *jāko* 'all', Malt. *paco* 'old (of animals)', *maqo* 'small, little, young' (< *maq-*, cf. *DED* 3768); *-ō* is found in Go. *punō* 'new' (*DED* 3511); *-e* occurs in Pa. Ga. (Oll.), Nk., cf. Pa. *capre* 'tasteless, insipid', Ga. (Oll.) *sapre 'id.'*, Nk. *sappe 'id.'*; *-u* occurs e.g. in Pengo cf. *jilu* 'cold', *vizu* 'all', *haru* 'small', *haṇku* 'straight' and in Malt., cf. *ēṛu* 'good, beautiful, in health' (<**eṛ-/*ēṛ-*, cf. Ta. *el̲-il, DED* 722).

2.1.4.3 Many adjective-derivational suffixes have the phonemic shape (C)-V̌C. This is a common case e.g. in Go. and Br., cf. the following instances: Go. *karkāl, kāriyal, kaṛiyal* (*DED* 1073 c **karV/*kār*) 'black', *kirkwāl* 'very thin', (*DED* 1326 **kir̲-*), *sarkal* (Y.) (besides *sarkō* and *sarko* in other dialects) 'straight' (*DEDS S* 371); the proposed connection with Pe. *haṇku* would show the root as **car-* and the derivational suffix as CV̌(C), i.e. **k V̌ (l)*; *visral* (Mu.) 'young' (cf. *visral marr* 'youngest son', *visro* 'younger', *DEDS S* 870), *pisal, pisol* 'mad' (*DEDS* 3407 < **pic-/*picc-*, cf. *DED* 3407), cf. Skt. *pitta-* 'bile'. In Br. the adjective-forming morpheme of the -(C)V̌C shape has the following phonemic forms: *-(k)un, -ēn; -ak;* cf. *k̲h̲īs-un* 'red' (PNDr **xēs*, PDr **ke-C/-*kē-C, DED* 1607), *ma-un* 'black,dark (of night)' (*DED* 3918), *mut-kun* 'old' (<**mut-, DED* 4057), *pūs-kun* 'new' (*DED* 3511); *kub-ēn* 'heavy' (< PNDr **kum-*, PDr **cum-, DED* 2204), *k̲h̲ar-ēn* 'bitter' (<PNDr **xaṭ-*, PDr **kaṭ-, DED* 952); *cun-ak* 'small' (*DED* 2135, cf. *cun-ā* 'child' <**cin-*); *pat-ak* 'short' (? *DED, DEDS* 3498).

2.1.5.1 Probably in all Dr. languages, a noun (in some languages in a form identical with the nominative, in some in the stem-form, in some modified by certain suffixes and/or morphophonemic rules) preceding another noun becomes the attribute: Ta. *kal* 'stone'+*uppu* 'salt'→ *kalluppu* 'stone-salt'; *talai* 'head'+ *nōvu* 'ache' → *talainōvu* 'head-ache'; Pa. *ēdir* 'hail' + *kel* 'stone' → *ēdirkel* 'hail-stone'. In some languages, the formal and semantic liaison between the two parts is strong enough to entitle us to speak about determinative compounds[30]: Ta. *maram* 'tree'+*peṭṭi* 'box'→ *marappeṭṭi* 'wooden box'; *veḷ* 'white'+*kal* 'stone'→ *veṇkal* 'quartz, white marble'.[31] The detailed investigation of such phenomena is outside the scope of this part of the morphology, and will form an integral portion of the third part on word-formation.

The substantives, as pointed out above, are often modified by suffixes; a typical example may be quoted from Koya: apart from what Tyler calls monomorphemic adjectives (like *nalla* 'black', *tella* 'white'), Koya has the following suffixes which derive 'derivative adjectives' from *nouns: -ana∾-anna, -atta, -al, -ti, -a, -i, -la*. Instances: *rūci→rūcanna* 'tasty', *balamu→balamatta* 'strong'.[32] Similar derivations may be attested from Old Ta., cf. *vāṉpuku talai-y-a kuṉṟam* (*Naṟṟiṇai* 347.4) 'the hill with the peak reaching the sky', *kaṟpiṉ nalaṅkēḻarivai* (*Kuṟ.* 338.7) 'the beautiful good woman of chastity',[33] or from Old Ma., cf. A.C. Sekhar *Evolution of Malayalam* (1953), 97. M.B. Emeneau deals with Kolami derivative adjectives on pp. 31-33 of his monograph *Kolami, a Dravidian Language* (1955), quoting forms like *vāḍi-ta* 'that which is in the garden' (<*vāḍi*), *rupial-a* 'which is worth (so-and-so many) rupees', *adavl-e* 'of them, belonging to them', *kis-ne* 'of the fire', or *lakḍe-ne* 'made of wood, wooden'.

2.1.5.2 There are (rare) cases that a particular form of an etymologically or semantically related group of adjectives, limited in its distribution *vis-à-vis* other forms, has been used as a part of a 'compound' which in such cases may indeed be classified as such since both formal and semantic criteria are strongly present: a telling example is the distinction in distribution and function between Ta. *ciṟu* (*DED* 1326, cf. *DED* 1308 Ta. *cil* and *DED* 2073 Ta. *ciṭṭu*) 'small', and Ta. *ciṉṉa* (*DED* 2135, cf. Ka. *ciṇi*, Kol. *sinnam* etc.)[34] 'small' : *ciṟu viral* 'little finger' : *ciṉṉa viral* 'a little finger, a small finger'. Out of the two etymologically unrelated (Ta. *ciṟu* < **kiṯ/u*: Ta. *ciṉṉa* < **ciṉ-*) but semantically 'identical' adjectives, it is exclusively the adj. *ciṟu* which forms compounds with specified meanings, cf. e.g. *ciṟucol*, lit. 'small talk'→'abuse', *ciṟunīr*, lit. 'small water'→'urine'.

2.1.5.3 In a few descriptions, a separate subclass of adjectives is distinguished and designated as 'adjectives of quantity and totality' (sometimes, this group is further subdivided). Thus, e.g., A.C. Sekhar's quoted description of Malayalam (1953) distinguishes adjectives of totality like *ellām* 'all' or *pala* 'many' (cf. *DED* 718 and 3289 resp.), and adjectives of quantity as *kāṇam* 'a measure of weight' (as in *añcu kāṇam poṉ* 'five *kāṇams* of gold'). All adjectives of quantity are in fact substantives. In the first group, *pala* 'many' behaves like any other adjective, so that it need to be (on formal grounds) separated from them, while *ellām* shows some tactic peculiarities and hence it should probably be treated separately. Cf. also, e.g., Kol. *itte* 'this much', etc. treated as 'numeral adjectives'.[36]

2.1.6 It has been argued from time to time that the indigenous Tamil grammatical tradition does not recognize the distinctive status of adjectives. It is true that, traditionally, 'adjectives' are 'derived' from nouns and/or verbs (in such traditional accounts, verbal relative participles are also treated as adjectives). However, in the classification of words (*col*) into main types, the question appears in a very different light.

With regard to the earliest Ta. grammar extant, the *Tolkāppiyam*, there can be no doubt that it does recognize adjectives.[37] In *Col. Peyar.* 158 and 159, *Tolkāppiyam* speaks about four kinds of *col*. In 158, it says that there are two (types of) words (*col*), viz. nouns (*peyar*) and verbs (*viṉai*). The next *sūtra* adds that the 'utterances [with, of] qualifiers (*uriccol*)' occur dependent on and along with the nouns and verbs. From this fact, as well as from *Col. Uri.* 297, it is obvious that *Tolk.* has in mind, when speaking about *uri-c-col*, the adjectives and the adverbs, i.e. 'qualifiers' of nouns and verbs. Further, *Tolk.* has four main chapters, dealing with nouns (*peyar*), verbs (*viṉai*), particles (*iṭai*) and qualifiers (*uri*) each. That he indeed means qualifiers by *uri-c-col,* and not stems or roots (as maintained e.g. by P.S. Subrahmanya Sastri who was inclined to equate Ta. *uriccol* with Skt. *dhātu*-!) is seen from *Col. Uri.* 297 where it is said that the *uriccoṟkiḷavi* 'when spread' is modified according to nouns and verbs along with which it occurs. Thus *uriccol* 'qualifiers' are subdivided into *peyar uriccol* or *adjectives* and *viṉai uriccol* or *adverbs.*

Tolkāppiyaṉ's analysis of qualifiers sounds in fact quite modern and again proves his remarkable insight and intuition when observing the facts of Tamil structure: though he classifies, in a way, 'particles' and 'qualifiers' together with 'nouns' and 'verbs' as the major word-classes (*col*), yet the status of dependence/independence (the features 'bound' vs. 'free') is, and very truly so, described as of a different degree for the first two (nouns, verbs) and for the second two (particles, qualifiers). For the 'modernity' of his classification of qualifiers in the light of comparative Dravidian cf. e.g. S.A. Tyler, *Koya* (1968), 68: "3.37. Qualifiers. Syntactically, qualifiers are attributive words preceding the noun or verb they qualify. Qualifiers agree with the head noun neither in person nor number. Qualifiers in attributive position to a noun are adjectives (Adj.), and those in attributive position to a verb are adverbs (Adv.)". This is a standpoint in fact entirely identical with *Tolkāppiyam's* conception of *uriccol* qualifying nouns (*peyar*) as adjectives (*peyaruriccol*) and verbs (*viṉai*) as adverbs (*viṉaiyuriccol*). It is in basic agreement with the linguistic facts of Tamil and Dravidian.

Therefore, it is incorrect to maintain that ancient Ta. grammarians did not recognize adjectives as such. *Tolkāppiyam* definitely distinguishes between adjectives (as a part of a larger syntactic class of qualifiers) and nouns (*peyar*); qualifiers are defined as syntactic class comprising adjectives and adverbs.

It is hoped that the preceding discussion will once for all show that we have to set up adjectives as a major word-class in our description of Dravidian languages.

NOTES

1 This is a definition of adjectives identical with that given first by M.B. Emeneau in *Kolami: A Dravidian Language* (1955), 31. Adjectives belong to a greater syntactic class of qualifiers (attributive words preceding the noun or verb they qualify). Qualifiers of nouns are adjectives, qualifiers of verbs are adverbs. This clear and simple conception of adjectives and adverbs seems to be the one most appropriate and workable for Dravidian. Cf. the lucid treatment of this class in S.A. Tyler, *Koya: An Outline Grammar (Gommu Dialect), UCLA* 54 (1969).

2 Contrary to the feeble defence of an untenable position by M. Andronov (in his *Tamil'skij jazyk* [1960] and *DJ* [1965]) who regards all adjectives in Dr. as derived from nouns or verbs.

3 M. Andronov, *DJ* (1965), 66. In spite of the attempts of some transformationalists to derive adjectives from underlying verbal or nominal forms, we agree with Jakobson that adjectives are linguistic primes the fundamental function of which is 'to qualify', 'to attribute' (Jakobson's lecture on children's language [Ann Arbor, April 11, 1969]). For a purely synchronic picture of the system of a Dr. language, cf. e.g. W. Bright's *An Outline of Colloquial Kannada* (1958), where the author gives the following classes: (1) Adjectives, such as *ī* 'this', *y/ellā* 'all'. (2) Nouns, such as *aṇṇa* 'elder brother', *cāk/u* 'knife'. (3) adverbs, such as *bega* quickly', *punha* 'again'. (4) Verbs, such as *māḍ/u* 'do', *kuḍi* 'drink' (5) Interjections, such as *hūⁿ* 'yes', *ayyō* 'alas' (p. 19).

4 Whereas Andronov would have us believe that it is verce versa, that adjectives were derived from nouns, cf. p. 56 of *DJ.* He would derive *ce-n-* in *centamiḻ* from *cemmai* and *naṉ-* in *naṉṉūl* from *naṉmai* (*DJ* 56). Even the morphophonemic rules (*sandhi*) show that this is exactly the reverse of the actual process (*nal+mai>naṉmai, nal+nūl>naṉṉūl,* and not *vice versa*).

5 A. Master, *JRAS* (1949), 106-107.

6 T. Burrow, *BSO[A]S, XII* : 1 (1947), 253-55.

7 Cf. *IHGTL* 15. As already pointed out, nouns, adjectives and verbs form one larger set – a NAV class based on similarities in syntactic patterns. According to Glazov in *IHGTL* 113-14, although he classifies adjectives as a separate part of speech, he derives them genetically from verbal/nominal roots. I find it difficult to agree with this conclusion, at least as far as a limited number of PDr adjective stems goes, and I find it quite impossible to agree with Andronov in his derivation of adjectives from abstract nouns.

8 "Including Kuruḵẖ" because the independent existence of primary adjectives, and even derived adjectives, has been strongly denied as far as Kuruḵẖ is concerned (cf. Andronov, *DJ*, 66).

9 A.C. Sekhar, *Evolution of Malayalam*, 93.

10 All instances from G.S. Gai, *Historical Grammar of Old Kannada* (Poona, 1946).

11 H.M.S. Nayak, *Kannada Literary* and *Colloquial*, 99.

12 *DED* 3513, Emeneau, *Kota Texts* I (1944), 22.

13 Bh. Krishnamurti and P. Sivananda Sarma, *A Basic Course in Modern Telugu* (1968), 18.

14 Cf. K. Mahadeva Satri, *Historical Grammar of Telugu* (1969), p. 251: "Like most pronominal and numeral roots there are also distinctive adjectival roots in Dravidian."

15 *The Pengo Language*, 44.

16 *The Parji Language*(1953), 32.

17 *Koya: An Outline Grammar* (*Gommu Dialect*) (1969).

18 F. Hahn, *Kuruḵẖ Grammar* (Calcutta, 1911), 145 and 150. For the connection between 'red' and 'blood', cf the usage in substandard Czech *červená* 'red (adj. fem.)' for *krev* 'blood'.

19 *The Brahui Language*, Part I (1909), 61.

20 The Modern Ta. instances from a treatise on prosody, *Yāppatikāram* (1961) by Pulavar Kuḻantai.

21 The Ma. instances from A.C. Sekhar, *Evolution*, 94, the Ka. instances from G.S. Gai, *Historical Grammar,* 71.

22 W.W. Winfield, *A Grammar of the Kui Language,* 43 and 165.

23 F. Hahn, *Kuruḵẖ Grammar*, 24 and Bray, *The Brahui Language* I, 84.

24 Stephen A. Tyler, *Koya: An Outline Grammar* (*Gommu Dialect*) (1969) 70-71 and 88-89.

25 An interesting entry (*DED* 3546) which shows that what is usually considered 'originally' a verb-stem from which adjectives and substantives were derived may rather be explained as an 'original' monomorphemic, even monosyllabic adjective stem, from which were derived the verbs and the substantives: Parji has prob. preserved the original monosyllabic root 'sour': *pul* (adj.); with the suffix *-a*, adjectives are formed in Pa. and Kuvi (Su.): *pul-l-a* 'sour'; further adjective formations: Pa. *pulla-ṭ, pul-di* 'sour', Ko. *puḷ-y 'id.'*, Tu. *puḷ-i 'id.'*, Te. *pul-i 'id.'*, Kol. *pul-l-e 'id.'*, Go. *pul-ā 'id.'*. Verbs are formed from this adjective base in many languages: Ta. *puḷ-i* 'to turn sour', Ko. *puḷ-y* 'to be sour', Pa. *pul-p-* 'to turn sour' etc.,and so are substantives, e.g. Ta. *puḷ-i* 'tamarind; acidity', To. *püḷ-y* 'tamarind', Tu. *puṇ-i-kè 'id.'*, Koṇḍa *pul-a* 'sour soup'. The Kuvi (Su.) *pulla mārnu* 'tamarind', lit. 'sour tree', shows that the adjective 'sour' is 'primary', 'earlier' than the substantive 'tamarind', though we might be tempted on semantic considerations to see the processes reversed.
26 These instances from *IHGTL* 148.
27 Cf. *periyam* 'we who (are) big', *Puṟam* 78.5.
28 The allomorph – historically probably later – of this 3. p.pl. *aḻriṇai* morpheme is *-a-v-ai*, cf. *alla* (*Tirukkuṟaḷ* 116.2)/*allavai*(*ibid.*96.1) 'those who are not so-and-so'.
29 Cf. M. Andronov, *Tamil'skij jazyk* (1960), 25, and *DJ* 63. While it is possible to further speculate about the etymological identity of this adjective derivational *-a* and the suffix of relative participle *-a*, there is a different morph *-a* occurring as the suffix of genitive-possessive, cf. OKa. *piriya keḻe-y-a* (10th cent.) 'of the big tank', OTa. *talai-y-a kuṉṟam* (*Naṟṟiṇai* 347.4) 'capped hill', *toḻil-a eḻili* (*ibid.*5.5) 'the cloud with (its) work'.
30 Of the type *'tatpuruṣa'* and *'karmadhāraya'*. Thus, e.g. M. Andronov in *DJ* 65, and J. Bloch, *SGD* 32..
31 A *syntactic class* of *qualifiers* is certainly something different from a *morphosyntactic category* of *adjectives*. In more traditional terminology, qualifiers or attributes form a constituent-class or a form-class which is dealt with in the 'section' on syntax; while adjectives are described to have a certain *form* and to perform a certain *function*. In Halliday's terminology, e.g., a qualifier (attribute in more traditional terms) is an instance of the category of *structure*, whereas an adjective is an instance of the category of *class*. Further one must object strongly against the statement made by Andronov on p. 65 of his *DJ* (1965). What he says is simply not true and hence his conclusion is quite false. After having described the use of substantive nouns in the adjective function, he goes on to say: "This way of the expression of the adjective meaning [*sic!*] is a general one in Dravidian languages, but in the most ancient Dravidian texts and, consequently, in Proto-Dravidian [*sic*!], it was the only possible way". Even a very quick and superficial examination of any 'ancient Dravidian text' will reveal a number of non-derived, 'primary' adjectives (i.e. items whose *form* and *function*, and – for the benefit of Andronov – whose *meanings* are quite distinct from and even in contrast with those of substantives): witness OTa. *peruviṟal* (*Puṟ.* 266.6) 'great strength' (*DED* 3613 Ta. *peru* adj. 'great'); *cil pōtu* (*Naṟ.* 42.9) 'few buds' (*DED* 1308), *cen nāy* (*ibid.*103.6) 'red dog' etc. etc.; OKa. *nalgiri* 'good mountain' (7th cent., *DED* 2986); OMa. *cem poṉ* 'red gold' (A.C. Sekhar, inscr. 5.24, 10th cent., *DED* 1607 Ta. *ce-, cem-* etc. 'red'.).
32 Cf. *Koya: An Outline Grammar,* 70-71.
33 For what happens in modern literary Tamil, cf. a brief but exact description in H. Beythan, *Praktische Grammatik der Tamilsprache* (1943), 131-134.
35 Cf. M.B. Emeneau, *Kolami* (1955), 32: "To *sinnam* 'small', which is of uncertain class, but probably an adjective, is added *-ta*, forming a derivative adjective *sinnamta*, from which is made the derivative noun *sinnamtad* 'that which is small'."
36 M.B. Emeneau, *Kolami, a Dravidian Language,* 31.
37 Those author who, like Andronov, let themselves be carried away by what is seemingly the traditional Tamil grammatical view, become victims of their own erronous interpretation of it.

BIBLIOGRAPHY

Agesthialingom, S.,
1964 "Tamil Nouns". *Anthropological Linguistics*, 6:1, 7-12.

Andronov, M.S.
1963 "Dravidian Languages", *Archiv Orientální*, 31:2, 177-197.
1965 *Dravidijskije jazyki* (Moskva).
1969 *A Standard Grammar of Modern and Classical Tamil* (Madras).

Bloch, J.,
1954 *Structure grammaticale des langues dravidiennes* (Paris, 1946; English translation by R.G. Harshe, Poona.

Burrow, T., and M.B. Emeneau,
1961 *A Dravidian Etymological Dictionary* (Oxford).
1968 *A Dravidian Etymological Dictionary-Supplement* (Oxford).

Caldwell, R.,
1913 *A Comparative Grammar of the Dravidian or South Indian Family of Languages* (1st ed. London, 1856, 2nd ed. London, 1875, 3rd ed. [revised by J.L. Wyatt and T. Ramakrisna Pillai] 1913).

Caṅka Ilakkiyam
1967 (edition of the texts of *Eṭṭuttokai* and *Pattuppāṭṭu* ed. by Es. *Vaiyāpuri Piḷḷai*), *Pāri Nilaiyam*, 2nd ed. (Madras, 1967).

Chafe, Wallace L.,
1970 *Meaning and the Structure of Language,* (Chicago and London).

Emeneau, M.B., *Kota Texts*
1944 *Kota Texts* I, (Berkeley and Los Angeles).
1955 *Kolami, a Dravidian Language* (Berkeley).
1957 "Numerals in Comparative Linguistics (with special reference to Dravidian)", *Bull. of the Inst. of History and Philosophy, Academia Sinica* 29, 1-10.
1962 *Brahui and Dravidian Comparative Grammar* (= *UCPL* 27) (Berkeley).
1961 "Brahui Demonstrative Pronouns", *JAS* III:1, 1-5.
1967 "The South Dravidian Languages", *JAOS* 87:4, 365-413.
1966 "Some South Dravidian Noun Formatives", *Ind. Linguistics* 27; issued Sept. 1968), 21-30.
1969 "Onomatopoetics in the Dravidian Linguistics Area", *Lg*. 45, 274-99.
1970 *Dravidian Comparative Phonology: A Sketch* (Annamalainagar).

Glazov, J.J.,
1962 "Morfemnyj sostav tamil'skogo klassicheskogo jazyka", *Narody Azii i Afriky* (Moskva, 3.
1962 *Morfologicheskij analiz klassicheskogo tamil'skogo jazyka* (Moskva).
1964 "Morfofonemika i sintaktofonemika klassicheskogo tamil'skogo jazyka (na materiale Tirukurala)", *Voprosy jazykoznanija* 3.
1964 "Sochetaemost' i porjadok morfem imennogo slovoobrazovanija v jazyke Tirukurala" *Kratkije soobshchenija Instituta narodov Azii Akad. nauk SSR*, 62.
1967 "Morphemic Analysis of the Language of Tirukkural", *IHGT* (Moscow), 113-76.

Grierson, G.A.,
1906 *Linguistic Survey of India* (= *Muṇḍā and Dravidian Languages,* by Sten Konow) (Calcutta).

Gundert, H.,
1962 *Malayāḷabhāṣāvyākaraṇam* (Kottayam).

Hockett, Ch.F.,
1947 "Problems of Morphemic Analysis", *Lg.* 23, 321-43.

Kandappa Chetty, K.,
1970 "Personal and Reflexive Pronouns in Dravidian", mimeographed (Annamalainagar).

Kedilaya, A.S.,
"Gender in Dravidian", *DL* 169-76.

Krishnamurti, Bh.,
1955 "The History of Vowel-Length in Telugu Verbal Bases", *JAOS* 75, 237-52.
1961 *Telugu Verbal Bases: A Comparative and Descriptive Study* (Berkeley).
1968 "Dravidian Personal Pronouns", *Studies in Indian Linguistics* (Annamalinagar-Poona), 189-205.
1969 "Comparative Dravidian Studies", *Current Trends in Linguistics* 5: *Linguistics in South Asia* (The Hague-Paris), 309-33.

Kushalappa, Gowda K.,
1963 "Descriptive Grammar of Vaḍḍārādhane", Unpublished dissertation (Annamalai University).
1968 "Gender Distinction in Gowda Kannada", *Studies in Indian Linguistics* (Annamalainagar-Poona), 212-22.

Mahadeva, Sastri K.,
1969 *Historical Grammar of Telugu* (Anantapur).

Meenakshisundaran, T.P.,
1965 *A History of Tamil Language* (Poona).

Narasimhachar, D.L. (ed.),
1959 *Śabdamaṇidarpaṇa* (Mysore).

Pavananti,
1946 *Naṉṉūl mūlamum Mayilaināṭaruraiyum,* ed. by U.Vē. Cāminat'aiyar (Madras).

Pike, K.L.,
1967 *Language in Relation to a Unified Theory of the Structure of Human Behaviour* (The Hague-Paris).

Radhakrishnan, R.,
1964 "Empty Morph and Sariyai", *Journ. of Annamalai University* 25, 115-20.
1963 "Tamil Numerals", *Ind. Linguistics* 24, 87-122.

Rajaraja, Varma, A.R.,
1970 *Kēraḷapāṇinīyam* (Kottayam).

Ramaswami, Aiyar, L.V.,
1928 "Notes on Dravidian", *Indian Historical Quarterly* 4.
1936 *The Evolution of Malayalam Morphology* (Ernakulam).

Shanmugam, S.V.,
1969 "Inflectional Increments in Dravidian", *DL* (Annamalainagar), 23-58.
1969 "Tamil Numerals", *Proceedings of the I. International Conference Seminar of Tamil Studies* II (Kuala Lumpur), 729-34.
1970 "Case System in Dravidian", mimeographed (Annamalainagar).
1971 *"Dravidian Nouns",* (Annamalainagar) (became accessible to me on Aug. 24, 1971, after the manuscript of this book was completed).

1968 "The Position of Tuḷu in Dravidian", *Ind. Linguistics* 29, 47-66.
1969 "The Gender and Number Categories in Dravidian, *Journal of Annamalai University* 26, 79-100.
1969 "The Central Dravidian Languages", *JAOS* 89:4, 739-50.

Subrahmanya, Sastri, P.S.,
1934 *History of Grammatical Theories in Tamil and Their Relation to the Grammatical Literature in Sanskrit* (Madras).

Tollkāppiyam-Collatikāram, ed.
1962-1963 SISS Works Publ. Soc. (Madras).

Willman-Grabówska, H.,
1952 "La catégorie du genre dans les langues dravidiennes", *Biuletyn polskiego towarzystwa językoznawczego* 11, 162-170.

Zvelebil, K.
1958 "Dative in Early Old Tamil", *IIJ* 54-65.
1962 "Personal Pronouns in Tamil and Dravidian'", *IIJ* 6, 65-69.
1967 "On the Monomorphemic Rules of Dravidian Bases", *Linguistics* 32, 87-95.
1967 "The Language of Peruṇkuṉṟūr Kiḻār", *IHGT* (Moscow), 11-109.
1970 *Comparative Dravidian Phonology* (The Hague-Paris).

INDEX

accusative, 27
accusative suffix, reconstruction, 31
adjectives
  complex, 59, 63-5
  definition of, 59
  demonstrative, 59
  descriptive, 59
  monomorphemic, 59
  monomorphemic demonstrative, 62-3
  numeral, 59
  primary descriptive, 60-1
  problem of, 59
adverbs, 67
agglutinative, 2
aḻriṇai, 9
amahat, 9
Andronov, 12, 15, 25, 48, 59

Bhattacharya, S. , 11, 12, 14, 35, 61
Bloch, J. , 11, 12, 14, 23, 24, 25, 27, 48, 50, 51, 60
Bray, Denys de, 83
Burrow, T. , 11, 12, 14, 35, 48, 60, 61

Caldwell, 11, 48
case, 9, 18
case-markers, in PDr., reconstruction, 33
case suffixes, 18
case-systems, 19
concord, 10
consonant clusters, 2

dative, reconstruction, 31
demonstrative, 38-39

echo-words, 6
Emeneau, M. B. , 11, 12, 17, 36, 44, 61, 63, 66
empty morphs, 18, 21, 23
enunciative-*u*, 2
exclusiveness, 6, 9

feminine, 10
Finck, 2
Friend-Pereira, 12, 36

Gai, G. S. , 40
gender, 9, 36
genitive markers, reconstruction, 31-32
Glazov, 26, 27, 48

Hahn, 51
Harshe, R. G. , 60

instrumental suffix, reconstruction, 32
interjections, 6
"internal fexion", 2
inclusiveness, 6, 9
inclusive-exclusive contrast, 36, 37, 38
indeclinables, 6
inflexional suffixes, 21, 23
  reconstruction in PDr., 22-23

Kandappa Chetty, M. , 40, 46, 47
Kēśirāja, 31
Krishnamurti, Bh. , 11, 12, 14, 37, 40, 44

Lazarus, 48
Letchmajee, 36
locative suffixes, reconstruction, 32

Mahābhāratam, 46
mahat, 9
masculine, 10
Master, A. , 48, 61
Meenakshisundaram, T. P. , 27
monosyllabicity of Dr. roots, 2

Nannaya, 46
Naṉṉūl, 40
nominative case, 23, 25, 27
noun, 2, 9 ff.
noun-inflection, 18
noun, in the attribute ('adjective') function, 65-6
number, 9, 12, 36
numerals, 33-36
  adjective, reconstruction, 34-5
  substantival, reconstruction, 36

oblique case, 23, 25, 27
oblique stem, 23
octogenal system, 36
onomatopoetics, 6

pāl, 10
parts-of-speech system, 2, 5-6, 7
person, 9, 36
personal nouns, 47-8
peyar, 19
plural, 12
plural suffix-reconstruction, 14-15, 17-18
Pope, 48
pronominal system - reconstructed, 46-7
pronominalized nouns, 47-8
    historical developments of, 49-50
    in CDr and NDr, 50-51
pronouns, personal, 36, 40
proximate -intermediate-distant, 38-39

Ramaswami, L. V. , 32
reflexive, 39-40
Rhenius, 48
root, 2

Sanskrit influence, 23
Subrahmanyam, P. S. , 12
Schlegel, 2
Sekhar, A. C. , 66
Shanmugam, S. V. ; 18, 26
singular, 12
sociative (comitative) marker, reconstruction, 33
stem-expansion, 19
Subrahmanya Sastri, P. S. , 67
substantives, 9 ff.
substitutes, 9
suffixation, 2
syllabic patterns of Dr. , 2
Systemzwang, 46

tiṇai, 10
Tirukkuṟaḷ, 25
Tiruvācakam, 49
Tolkāppiyam, 10, 19, 67
Trench, 50
Tyler, S. A. , 50, 61, 63, 66, 67

uri, 67
uriccol, 67
uyartiṇai, 9, 10

Vaḍḍārādhane, 31
verb, 2
viḻi, 19
Vīracōḻiyam, 40

Winfield, 24, 61